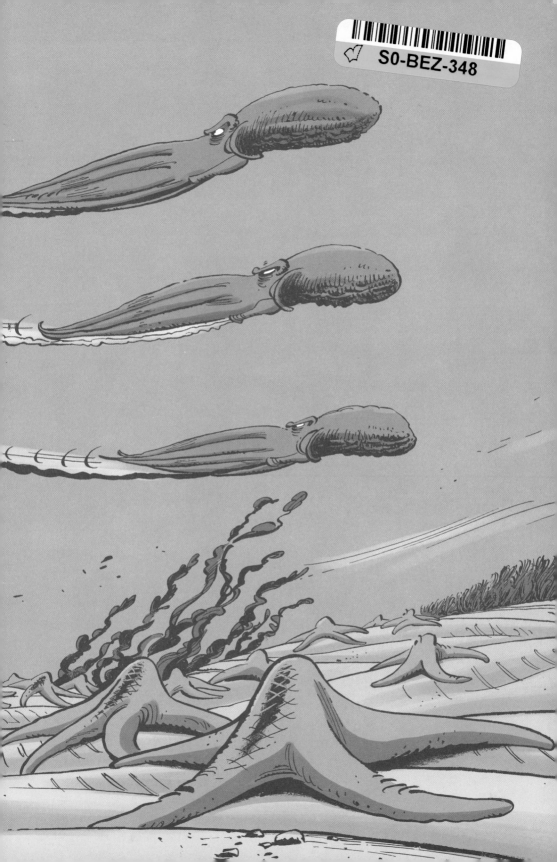

sea creatures

in their own words

2. ARMED & DANGEROUS

Christophe Cazenove
Writer

Jytéry
Artist

Alexandre Amouriq & Mirabelle
Colorists

PAPERCUTZ
New York

THREATENED SPECIES RATINGS

Here are various statuses that the International Union for the Conservation of Nature (IUCN) assigns to species, which you'll find used about different sea creatures in these pages. The IUCN evaluates species in terms of several criteria, such as population size, habitat destruction, number of individuals that have reached sexual maturity, etc.

NE: Not evaluated—no data to allow the species to be evaluated according to the criteria.
DD: Data Deficient — data does not allow for evaluation.
LC: Least Concern — this is where we put species that have been evaluated but that don't go into the categories below. Humans fit in here.
NT: Near Threatened — close to fulfilling all the criteria to become threatened in the near future.
VU: Vulnerable — facing an elevated risk of extinction in the wild.
EN: Endangered — very high risk of extinction in the wild.
CR: Critically Endangered — extremely high risk of endangerment in the wild.
EW: Extinct in the Wild — lost species that only exists in cultivation.
CO: Collapse — assigned to ecosystems that have collapsed throughout their distribution.
EX: Extinct — species has completely vanished.

A big thank you to Michele Hignette.

—Christophe

I'm dedicating this graphic novel to all nature lovers, and especially to those who love the ocean depths. Thank you, Alexandre and Mirabelle, for their magnificent colors.

—Jytéry

SEA CREATURES IN THEIR OWN WORDS
Les Animaux Marins en Bande Dessinee [Sea Creatures in Comics] by Cazenove and Jytéry © 2014 BAMBOO ÉDITION.
www.bamboo.fr
All other editorial material © 2017 by Papercutz.

**SEA CREATURES IN THEIR OWN WORDS #2
"ARMED & DANGEROUS"**
Christophe Cazenove – Writer
Thierry Jytéry – Artist
Alexandre Amouriq & Mirabelle – Colors
Nanette McGuinness – Translation
Tom Orzechowski – Letterer
Big Bird Zatryb – Production
Dawn Guzzo – Production Coordinator
Robert V. Conte – Editor
Jeff Whitman – Assistant Managing Editor
Jim Salicrup
Editor-in-Chief

ISBN: 978-1-62991-743-6

Printed in China
May 2017

Papercutz books may be purchased for business or promotional use. For information on bulk purchases please contact Macmillan Corporate and Premium Sales Department at (800) 221-7945 x5442.

Distributed by Macmillan
First Papercutz Printing

SEA CREATURES IN THEIR OWN WORDS graphic novels are also available digitally wherever e-books are sold.

www.papercutz.com

THE CLOWN FISH AND ITS BUDDY, THE ANEMONE

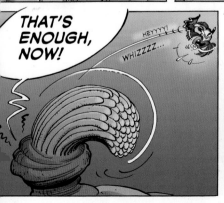

THE PARROTFISH

THE **PARROTFISH** OWES ITS NAME TO ITS SPARKLING COLORS...

...AND FROM ITS MOUTH, WHICH IT USES TO SCRAPE THE SURFACE OF CORAL-- WHICH IS WHAT IT EATS!

SCRATCH SCRATCH SCRATCH SCRATCH SCRATCH SCRATCH SCRATCH SCRATCH SCRATCH SCRATCH SCRATCH SCRATCH SCRATCH SCRATCH SCRATCH SCRATCH

OH, THAT'S ENOUGH OF THAT **RACKET!**

ITS TEETH CRUSH THE BITS OF CORAL...

CRACK CRACK CRACK CRACK CRACK CRACK CRACK CRACK

OKAY, OKAY, I GET IT. I'M OUT OF HERE!

...WHICH, ONCE DIGESTED, COME BACK OUT AGAIN IN THE FORM OF VERY WHITE, VERY FINE SAND!

POOFT

HEY, I'M RIGHT HERE!

DEPENDING ON THE SPECIES, IT PRODUCES TENS OF HUNDREDS OF POUNDS OF SAND A YEAR...

HELP!

IT'S SAID THAT WITHOUT THEM, THE SANDY WHITE ISLANDS IN THE TROPICS WOULDN'T EVEN EXIST...

HEY... B-BUT?!

...AND FINALLY, IT'S VERY BAD-TEMPERED!

THIS IS A **PRIVATE** BEACH--**GET OUT!**

WHA--? FINE!

WE'RE NOT DOING ANYTHING WRONG HERE...

PARROTFISH
Scaridae sp.

- SIZE: 20-130 centimeters [8-51 inches], depending on the species
- DIET: Herbivore and reef scavenger
- DISTINCTIVE FEATURE: At night it sometimes wraps itself up in a cocoon of mucus that takes a half hour to produce.

DEPTH: 1-30 METERS [3-99 FEET]	NT*	GEOGRAPHIC LOCATION

*THREATENED SPECIES RATING. SEE THE TABLE ON PAGE TWO

THE MIMIC OCTOPUS

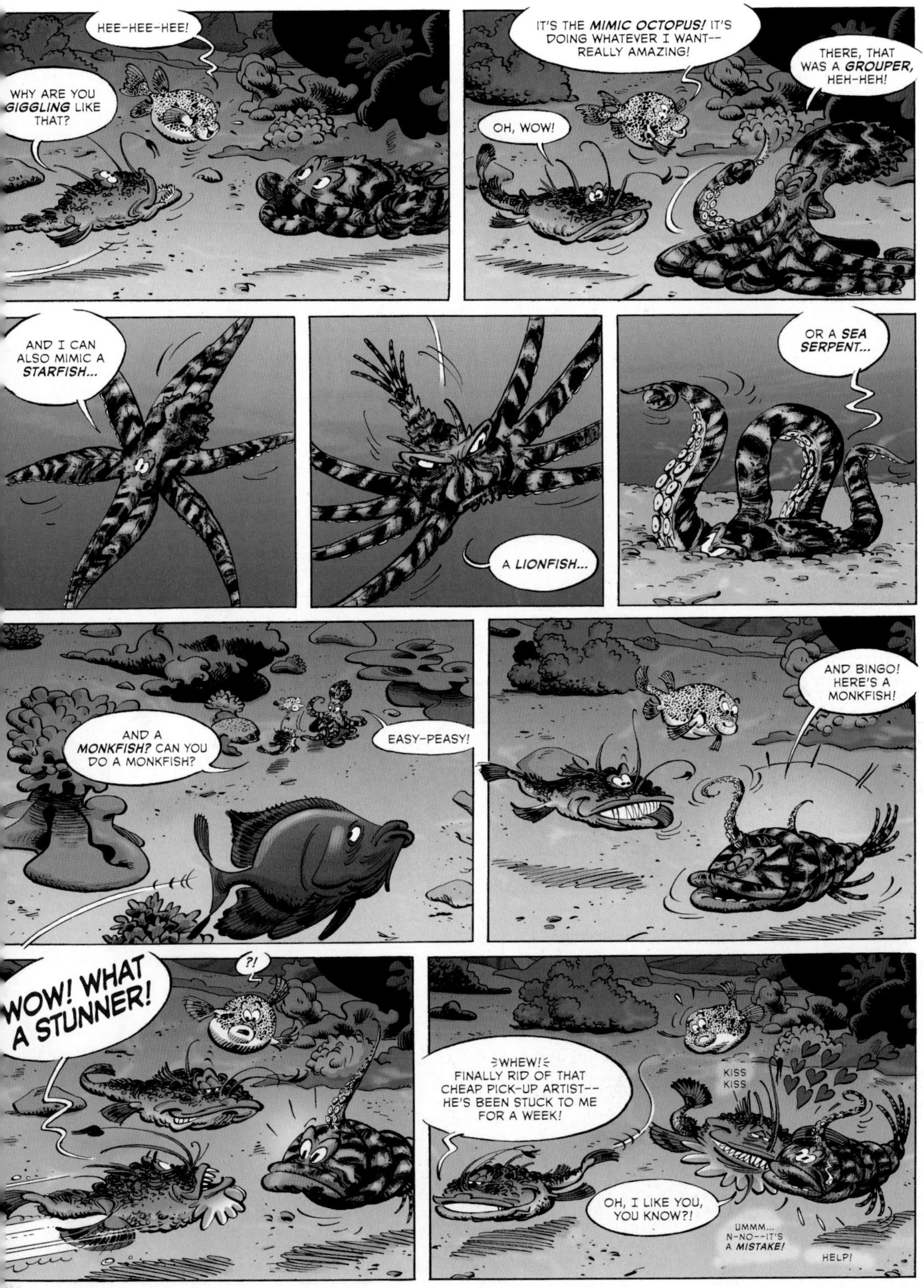
HEE-HEE-HEE!
WHY ARE YOU GIGGLING LIKE THAT?
IT'S THE MIMIC OCTOPUS! IT'S DOING WHATEVER I WANT-- REALLY AMAZING!
THERE, THAT WAS A GROUPER, HEH-HEH!
OH, WOW!
AND I CAN ALSO MIMIC A STARFISH...
A LIONFISH...
OR A SEA SERPENT...
AND A MONKFISH? CAN YOU DO A MONKFISH?
EASY-PEASY!
AND BINGO! HERE'S A MONKFISH!
WOW! WHAT A STUNNER!
?!
WHEW! FINALLY RID OF THAT CHEAP PICK-UP ARTIST-- HE'S BEEN STUCK TO ME FOR A WEEK!
KISS KISS
OH, I LIKE YOU, YOU KNOW?!
UMMM... N-NO--IT'S A MISTAKE!
HELP!

THE SIZE OF THE IGUANA

IT'S NOT AT ALL EASY FOR THE **MARINE IGUANA** TO FEED ITSELF...

I'M **STARVING**!

ME, TOO!

WILL YOU TELL ME IF YOU FIND SOMETHING?

AAARGHHH

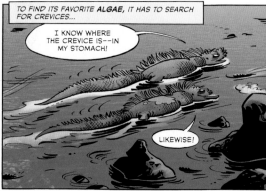

TO FIND ITS FAVORITE **ALGAE**, IT HAS TO SEARCH FOR CREVICES...

I KNOW WHERE THE CREVICE IS--IN MY STOMACH!

LIKEWISE!

...FIGHT AGAINST THE FORCE OF THE CURRENT...

SAVE ME A LITTTTTTLE-- --EH? **AAAAAAAH**

YEAH, YEAH,

DON'T WORRY!

...AND THEN DIVE FOR ABOUT 30 MINUTES TO NIBBLE ON A LITTLE BIT, IN A SEA THAT'S OFTEN **FREEZING**!

OH, DEAR-- THAT'S ALL THAT'S LEFT!

WHEN IT CAN'T FIND ANY FOOD, THE MARINE IGUANA HAS TO SHRINK ITS BODY SO IT WON'T SUFFER FROM **HUNGER**...

THERE'S NOTHING LEFT TO NOSH ON!

WE'LL GET THROUGH IT VIA **"BELT" MODE**!

AGAIN?! BUMMER...!

...IT LOSES UP TO 20% OF ITS ORIGINAL WEIGHT...

THE BRIGHT SIDE...

...IS THAT WE REDISCOVER OUR MODEL FIGURE! RIGHT, LADIES?

NOW, THAT'S AN IGUANA!

OOOHH! WHAT A GUY!

ARF-- ARF!

...AND, INCREDIBLY ENOUGH, A LITTLE BIT OF ITS CARTILAGE SHRINKS!

WELL, THAT DEPENDS ON THE IGUANA!

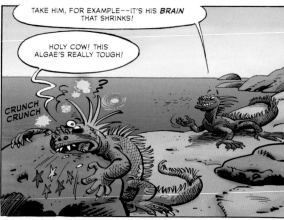

TAKE HIM, FOR EXAMPLE--IT'S HIS **BRAIN** THAT SHRINKS!

HOLY COW! THIS ALGAE'S REALLY TOUGH!

CRUNCH CRUNCH

A CUTTLEFISH THAT CAN DEFEND ITSELF

THE **CUTTLEFISH** HAS A BLACK BELT IN SELF DEFENSE!

WHO GOES THERE?

KEE-AI!

IT HAS MANY WAYS OF ESCAPING ITS PREDATORS...

OH, NO-- THIS **SEA BASS** IS STRONG... ⸮GULP!⸮

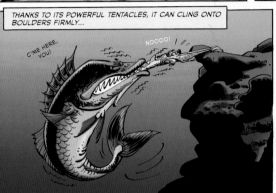

THANKS TO ITS POWERFUL TENTACLES, IT CAN CLING ONTO BOULDERS FIRMLY...

C'ME HERE, YOU!

NOOOO!

...AND EVEN IF IT CAN'T SLIP IN EVERYWHERE, LIKE THE **OCTOPUS**...

SNIFF-- SNIFF-- SNIFF--

...IT HAS AN **INK SAC**, WHICH IT EXPELS AT WILL!

FWOOSSSHHH

THIS CLOUD COVERS ITS ESCAPE, IRRITATES ITS PREDATOR'S EYES AND DISTURBS ITS SENSE OF SMELL!

ACHOO- ACHOO

THE PROBLEM FOR THE CUTTLEFISH, HOWEVER...

TAKE THAT... AND THAT!

FWOOSSHH

...IS WHEN TO KNOW HOW TO USE ITS DEFENSE METHODS-- IN THE RIGHT ORDER...

HEH-HEH!

HEH-HEH!

I'M A **LOSER**! I FORGOT TO PICK OUT A **HIDEOUT** FIRST!

HEH-HEH!

THE MANDARINFISH

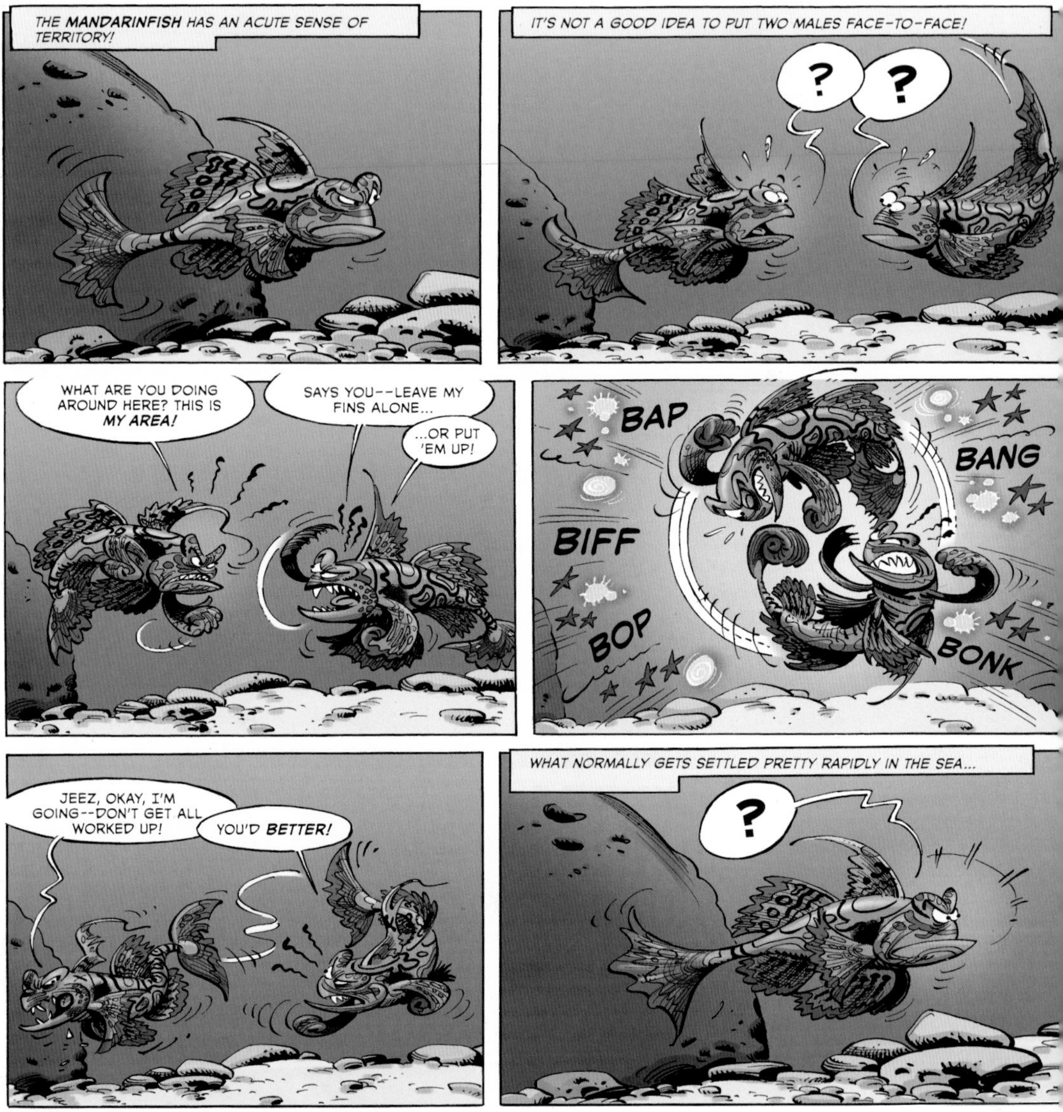

THE MANDARINFISH HAS AN ACUTE SENSE OF TERRITORY!
IT'S NOT A GOOD IDEA TO PUT TWO MALES FACE-TO-FACE!
?
?
WHAT ARE YOU DOING AROUND HERE? THIS IS MY AREA!
SAYS YOU--LEAVE MY FINS ALONE...
...OR PUT 'EM UP!
BAP
BANG
BIFF
BOP
BONK
JEEZ, OKAY, I'M GOING--DON'T GET ALL WORKED UP!
YOU'D BETTER!
WHAT NORMALLY GETS SETTLED PRETTY RAPIDLY IN THE SEA...
?

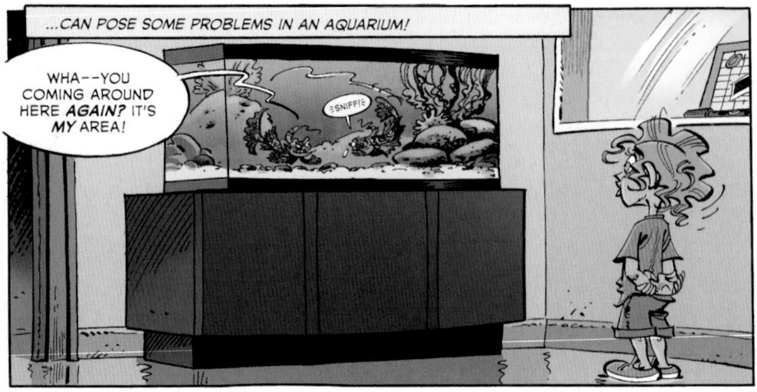

...CAN POSE SOME PROBLEMS IN AN AQUARIUM!
WHA--YOU COMING AROUND HERE AGAIN? IT'S MY AREA!
SNIFF!

MANDARINFISH

Synchiropus splendidus

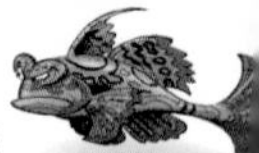

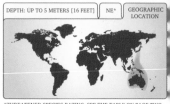

•SIZE: 5-8 centimeters [2-3 inches]

•DIET: Carnivore

•DISTINCTIVE FEATURE: When the size of an aquarium is smaller than two territories, there's not enough room for two males. Hence, a brawl!

DEPTH: UP TO 5 METERS [16 FEET]	NE*	GEOGRAPHIC LOCATION

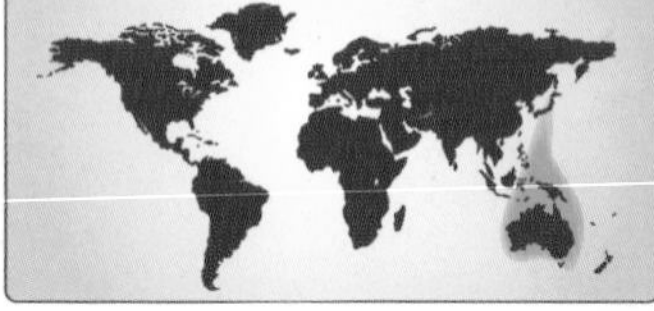

*THREATENED SPECIES RATING. SEE THE TABLE ON PAGE TWO.

THE SEADRAGON

SEA DRAGONS...? ALIVE?!

WHY, YES! HERE ALONG THE AUSTRALIAN COASTLINE, YOU CAN RUN INTO A FEW--

WELL, LOOK HERE...

THIS IS THE COMMON SEA DRAGON, *PHYLLOPTERYX!*

IT LOOKS LIKE A SEAHORSE.

YES, EXCEPT ITS TAIL ISN'T *"PREHENSILE."* IT CAN'T CLING ONTO ROCKS OR PLANTS.

PHOOEY-- WHAT A *LOSER!*

THIS IS THE *LEAFY SEA DRAGON!*

CRAZY--IT LOOKS LIKE SOME ALGAE WITH FINS!

THAT'S PART OF ITS CAMOUFLAGE! IT CAN EVEN CHANGE COLOR!

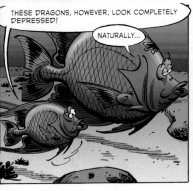

THESE DRAGONS, HOWEVER, LOOK COMPLETELY DEPRESSED!

NATURALLY...

...HAVE YOU EVER TRIED SPITTING OUT FLAMES UNDERWATER?

HA-HA-HA-HA!

PSHOO

PSHOO

9

THE STINGRAY

LET'S OBSERVE THE **STINGRAY'S** HUNTING TECHNIQUE...

IT SENSES THE MAGNETIC FIELD EMITTED BY **MOLLUSKS** HIDDEN UNDER THE SAND...

HEH-HEH-HEH!

UH-OH! SOMETHING'S THERE!

≥GULP!≤

HIDE SO IT'LL COME BACK ANOTHER TIME!

TO FLUSH THEM OUT INTO THE OPEN, IT FLAPS ITS FINS...

FLOOP FLOOP

FLOOP FLOOP

...IN ORDER TO WHIP UP AS MUCH SAND AS POSSIBLE!

????????

IT'S REALLY AN EFFICIENT TECHNIQUE!

YUM!

CRACK!

CRUNCH!

EEEEK

HELP!

A UFO?!

EFFICIENT? EFFICIENT? THAT REMAINS TO BE **SEEN!**

?!

HMMM... THE **SEA WHIP** DOESN'T SEEM TO AGREE...

THAT'S BECAUSE IT'S NOT THE ONE THAT HAS TO CLEAN UP AFTERWARDS!

OOPS... SORRY!

STINGRAY
Taenriura lymma

·SIZE: Up to 2 meters [7 feet]

·DIET: Carnivore

·DISTINCTIVE FEATURE: There are over 100 species of poisonous rays. They're pleasant animals, I'm telling you!

DEPTH: 5-200 METERS [16-656 FEET]	NT*	GEOGRAPHIC LOCATION

*THREATENED SPECIES RATING. SEE THE TABLE ON PAGE TWO.

10

THE PIKE'S PLACE

THAT'S WHAT YOU CALL "HIDING" YOURSELF...?
YOU'RE A *DISGRACE TO PIKES!*

SORRY, DADDY!
HEH-HEH!

I'M GOING TO SHOW YOU HOW WE'VE HUNTED SINCE
TIME IMMEMORIAL!

FOLLOW ME!

YES, DADDY!

FOR A START, YOU PICK A CALM RIVER BASIN, WITH
A CURTAIN OF AQUATIC PLANTS...

IT'S PERFECT
HERE!

IF THERE ARE SOME ROOTS AND HOUSEHOLD GARBAGE,
THAT'S EVEN BETTER!

DO YOU SEE
ME HERE?

UMM... NO,
DADDY!

SCOOT! A *BOTTOM-FEEDER* IS APPROACHING!

WATCH IT...

READY TO POUNCE...

ATTACK--

OUCH!

HUMPH!

🌿🌀★‼
ROOTS!

🌀★⚡‼
PLANTS!

...AFTER ALL, IT'S A PERFECT HIDING PLACE!

OKAY,
DADDY!

HEE-
HEE!

11

THE ZEBRA MANTIS SHRIMP

I'M HUNGRY!

THE **ZEBRA MANTIS SHRIMP** IS ONE OF THE--

CHOK

BLURP

WOOOEFFF

--FASTEST PREDATORS IN THE WORLD!

LET'S PLAY THAT SCENE AGAIN IN SLOW MOTION...

CHOK

AAARGHH

IT MUST BE SAID THAT THE ZEBRA MANTIS SHRIMP LAUNCHES ITS CLAWS IN TWO-THOUSANDTHS OF A SECOND!

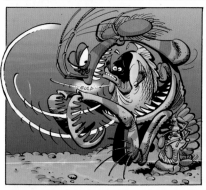

GULP

SMACK
CRACK GULP
SMACK CHEW
SLURP
SMACK YUM
CRACK

BLURP!

THE SNAG WHEN YOU CATCH YOUR PREY SO QUICKLY...

...IS THAT YOU DON'T EVEN REMEMBER IT ANYMORE!

I'M HUNGRY!

ZEBRA MANTIS SHRIMP
Lysiosquillina maculata

·SIZE: Up to 200 centimeters [8 Inches]

·DIET: Carnivore

·DISTINCTIVE FEATURE: Look no further for which creature has the best color vision in the animal world: it's this one!

| DEPTH: 3-40 METERS [10-131 FEET] | NE* | GEOGRAPHIC LOCATION |

*THREATENED SPECIES RATING. SEE THE TABLE ON PAGE TWO.

SPONGE & CO.

THE OCEANS ARE FILLED WITH LIVING ORGANISMS...

...THAT DON'T LOOK LIKE LIVING ORGANISMS AT ALL!

HELLO!

HOW'S IT GOING?

SO, HOW'S IT HANGING, FRIENDS?

A LITTLE HUMID, DON'T YOU THINK?

THIS INCLUDES THE **SPONGE**, ONE OF THE MOST PRIMITIVE ANIMALS WITH A VERY SIMPLE STRUCTURE!

HEY! IF IT'S SO SIMPLE, WHY CAN'T **YOU** DO THE SAME THING?!

AND ALSO **CORALS**...

ARE YOU **SURE** YOU'RE A CORAL?

WHOA! YOU'RE NOT GOING TO **START**, EH?

UH...WELL, YOU'RE NOT SO TERRIBLE LOOKING!

BRYOZOANS...

YOU CAN CALL ME "BRYO!"

IT'S EASIER!

SEA CUCUMBERS, TUNICATES...

ARE YOU GOING TO **MOVE** TODAY?

DON'T FEEL LIKE IT!

...WITH LOTS OF INTERESTING THINGS FOR US TO LEARN FROM THEM!

DO YOU KNOW THE ONE ABOUT THE WHELK AND THE SCALLOP?

HAH-HAH-HAH!

THAT BEING SAID, THERE ARE THINGS OTHER THAN LIVING ORGANISMS UNDERWATER...

...BECAUSE, AUNTIE AGATHA, WHO LEFT FOR THE SOUTHERN SEAS... BLAH... BLAH... BLAH...

...PERHAPS WE SHOULD TELL HIM THAT HE'S TALKING TO A **ROCK BEAST!**

AND BLAH-BLAH-BLAH-BLAH-BLAH-BLAH-BLAH-BLAH-BLAH...

DO FISH GET THIRSTY?

THE *FIVE-DOLLAR* QUESTION: *DO FISH DRINK?*

IF YOU GET IT RIGHT, I'LL GET YOU A LITTLE CUP OF COFFEE, HEE-HEE!

SINCE FISH ARE IMMERSED IN WATER INSIDE AND OUTSIDE OF THEIR BODIES, THEY'RE CONDEMNED TO DRINK-- BUT NOT IN THE SAME WAY WE DO!

GLUG GLUG GLUG GLUG

YEAH! FOR US, IT'S *UNLIMITED* DRINKS!

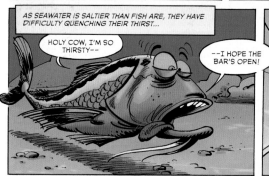

AS SEAWATER IS SALTIER THAN FISH ARE, THEY HAVE DIFFICULTY QUENCHING THEIR THIRST...

HOLY COW, I'M SO THIRSTY--

--I HOPE THE BAR'S OPEN!

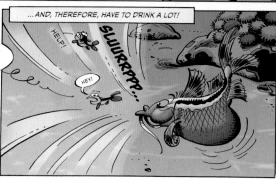

...AND, THEREFORE, HAVE TO DRINK A LOT!

HELP!

SLUURRPPP...

HEY!

SURPRISINGLY THOUGH, FRESHWATER FISH ARE SALTIER THAN THE WATER THEY SWIM IN...

?

SLUURRP!

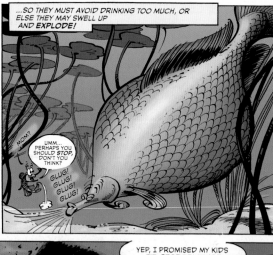

...SO THEY MUST AVOID DRINKING TOO MUCH, OR ELSE THEY MAY SWELL UP AND *EXPLODE!*

MOM?

UMM... PERHAPS YOU SHOULD *STOP*, DON'T YOU THINK?

GLUG! GLUG! GLUG! GLUG!

AND THEN THERE ARE THE OTHERS...

I JUST SPENT A FEW WEEKS IN FRESH WATER--

OH, YEAH?

YEP, I PROMISED MY KIDS I'D *STOP* DRINKING!

THE REMORA

YOU GAVE ME THE CHOICE, I'D LOVE TO HAVE A *SUCTION CUP!*

HUH? ARE YOU SICK, OR WHAT?!

IT WOULD BE GREAT! ARE YOU FAMILIAR WITH THE *REMORA?* IT'S OBVIOUSLY GOT ONE ON ITS HEAD!

WELL, THAT MUST LOOK CLEVER!

THANKS TO THAT, THE REMORA CAN STICK ITSELF TO OTHER FISH OR ONTO THE HULL OF A BOAT...

AH! THERE'S THE *8:45 SHARK!*

...AND TRAVEL WITHOUT IT COSTING A DIME!

SCHLUB

AND OFF WE GO!

THE *OCTOPUS* USES ITS ROWS OF SUCTION CUPS TO CRAWL...

SCHLUB SCHLUB SCHLUB SCHLUB SCHLUB SCHLUB SCHLUB SCHLUB

...CATCH ITS PREY, AND EVEN TO DEFEND ITSELF!

EEEEK!

NO!

ARG...!

IT'S MINE!

BEAT IT!

YES, BUT DON'T TIRE YOURSELF OUT. I'M GOOD WITH SUCTION CUPS!

OH, YEAH?

MY WIFE'S KISSES...!

THERE YOU ARE! WHERE'VE YOU BEEN, MY LOVE?

SMACK SMACK SMACK SMACK SMACK SMACK SMACK SMACK

WATCH OUT FOR THE CONE

WHERE DO WE FIND THOSE FAMOUS CONES, DADDY?

HEY! WAIT, WAIT!

FIRST OF ALL, YOU NEED TO KNOW TWO OR THREE LITTLE THINGS ABOUT THIS ESPECIALLY POISONOUS *SHELLFISH!*

OH?!

FOR A START, IT'S RECOMMENDED THAT YOU PUT ON GOOD GLOVES BEFORE STICKING YOUR HAND INTO THE SAND!

"NEXT, GRAB IT FROM THE BIG END TO AVOID ITS STINGER ON THE POINTED END!

SSSNOORREEE...

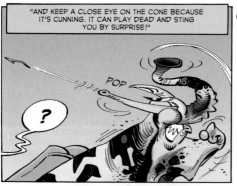

"AND KEEP A CLOSE EYE ON THE CONE BECAUSE IT'S CUNNING. IT CAN PLAY DEAD AND STING YOU BY SURPRISE!"

POP

?

IT'S ALSO BEST TO KNOW THAT ITS STINGER CAN PIERCE SOME FABRICS AND PLASTICS!

WELL, THEN--THA BEAST!

BUT ABOVE ALL, IT'S BETTER NOT TO TAKE RISKS FOR NO REASON!

COME ON, LET'S GO OBSERVE THE HARMLESS, PRETTY MUSSELS OVER THERE INSTEAD!

YACK-YACK-YACK!

HOME-SHARING

HELLO? YOU LIVE WITH *SNAPPING SHRIMP...?*

WELL, YEAH, LIKE MOST *GOBIES!*

ARE THEY THE ONES THAT DIG YOUR BURROW?

YES, THEY ALSO CLEAN IT BY THROWING THE SAND AND DEBRIS OUTSIDE!

SCRATCH SCRATCH SCRATCH...

WE'RE HOME-SHARING. ON THEIR SIDE, THEY MAINTAIN OUR SHELTER...

...AND SINCE THEY'RE *BLIND,* I WARN THEM WHEN THERE'S DANGER. THAT'S WHY ONE OF THEIR ANTENNAS TOUCHES ME CONSTANTLY...

B-BUT, WHY DIDN'T YOU WARN THEM?

SQUEAK YUM SCRUNCH SQUEAK-EEEE

AIEEEEE

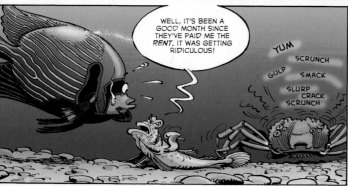

WELL, IT'S BEEN A GOOD MONTH SINCE THEY'VE PAID ME THE *RENT.* IT WAS GETTING RIDICULOUS!

YUM SCRUNCH GULP SMACK SLURP CRACK SCRUNCH

DJEDDAH SNAPPING SHRIMP
Alpheus djeddensis

- SIZE: Up to 4 centimeters [1.6 inches]

- DIET: Crustaceans, zooplankton

- DISTINCTIVE FEATURE: A real brain buster, the genus Alpheus brings together over 80 species of seawater shrimp.

| DEPTH: 5-20 METERS [16-65 FEET] | NE* | GEOGRAPHIC LOCATION |

*THREATENED SPECIES RATING. SEE THE TABLE ON PAGE TWO.

THE LOBSTER'S PAIN

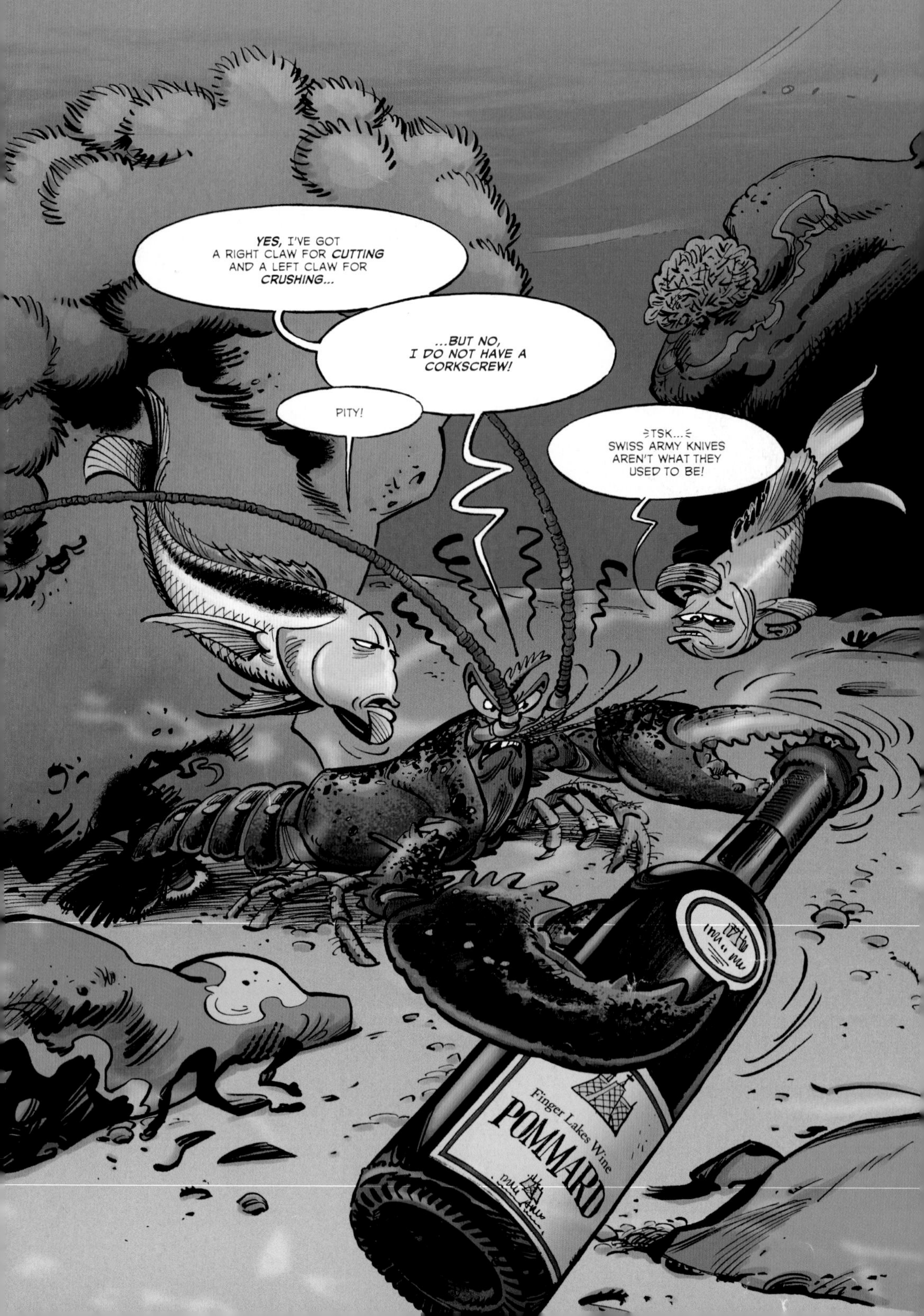
YES, I'VE GOT A RIGHT CLAW FOR CUTTING AND A LEFT CLAW FOR CRUSHING...
...BUT NO, I DO NOT HAVE A CORKSCREW!
PITY!
TSK... SWISS ARMY KNIVES AREN'T WHAT THEY USED TO BE!
Finger Lakes Wine
POMMARD

THE SPIDER CRAB

THE **SPIDER CRAB** HAS A PARTICULARLY STURDY SHELL...

BANG BANG BANG

ALRIGHT, ALREADY! YOU'RE GOING TO HURT YOURSELF DOING THAT!

ALAS, AS IS THE CASE FOR ALL CRABS, THE SHELL DOESN'T GROW WITH THE REST OF ITS BODY...

YOU LOOK A BIT LIKE A STUFFED SAUSAGE IN THERE...

OH, REALLY? DO YOU THINK SO?!

THIS IS WHY THEY HAVE TO MOLT, THAT IS TO SAY, LEAVE ITS PROTECTION WHEN IT HAS BECOME TOO TIGHT...

≥HMPPHHH!≤

...AND WAIT UNTIL THE NEW ONE HARDENS! DURING THIS TIME, THE **SEA SPIDER** IS NO LONGER PROTECTED...

OH, MY--THE **SHAME!**

LOOK AT THE CUTE LITTLE ONE!

THEN, WHEN ITS NEW SHELL HAS GROWN TOO SMALL AGAIN, IT WILL HAVE TO EXCHANGE IT AGAIN... AND AGAIN...

I REALLY HAVE TO STOP EATING SWEET TRASH!

CRABS SOMETIMES HAVE FOUND A SOLUTION TO THIS ISSUE...

YES--YES--YES! I'VE SOLVED THE PROBLEM!

?

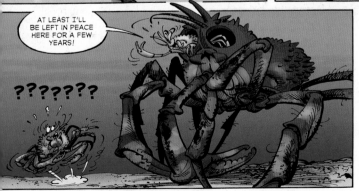

AT LEAST I'LL BE LEFT IN PEACE HERE FOR A FEW YEARS!

??????

SPIDER CRAB
Maja brachydactyla

- SIZE: Up to 20 centimeters long and 15 centimeters wide [8 inches long and 6 inches wide]
- DIET: Omnivore
- DISTINCTIVE FEATURE: It molts 11-13 times during its first year. Now that's growth!

DEPTH: UP TO 50 METERS [3-164 FEET]	NE*	GEOGRAPHIC LOCATION

*THREATENED SPECIES RATING. SEE THE TABLE ON PAGE TWO.

THE VELVET CRAB

TAKE A WALK ALONG THE BRITTANY COAST AT LOW TIDE...

DID'JA REMEMBER TO TAKE OUT THE TRASH?

OOPS! I ALMOST FORGOT...

...AND WATCH A *VELVET CRAB* LEAVE ITS HIDEOUT...

CLICK
CLICK
CLICK

THIS LITTLE CRAB LOVES GARBAGE...

NICE! THE TOURISTS LEFT ME LOTS OF GRUB AGAIN!

TOO KIND!

...AND ALSO DEAD ANIMALS...

SHRIMP, SEA URCHINS, SHELLFISH...

I'M SO *SPOILED* TODAY!

ACTUALLY, MANY SPECIES OF CRABS FEED ON DEAD BODIES!

YES, BUT IF YOU'VE GOT A FRESH OYSTER, I'M NOT AGAINST IT, EH?

CRUNCH GNAW

CHOMP

THIS WAY, THE VELVET CRAB CONTRIBUTES TO CLEANING UP THE BEACHES...

AND THERE YOU ARE! I'M DONE WITH MY DAY!

AS A RESULT, IT'S NOT UNUSUAL TO HEAR THE FEMALE CALLING THE MALE...

DID YOU REMEMBER TO BRING THE TRASH CANS BACK IN?

OOPS! I ALMOST FORGOT...

VELVET CRAB
Necora puber

- SIZE: 5-10 centimeters [2-4 inches]
- DIET: Scavenger omnivore
- DISTINCTIVE FEATURE: With its 5-tooth shell and red eyes, it's a real knockout!

| DEPTH: 10-70 METERS [32-230 FEET] | NE* | GEOGRAPHIC LOCATION |

*THREATENED SPECIES RATING. SEE THE TABLE ON PAGE TWO.

DIFFICULT NAMES

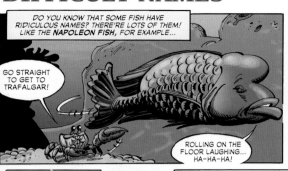

DO YOU KNOW THAT SOME FISH HAVE RIDICULOUS NAMES? THERE'RE LOTS OF THEM! LIKE THE **NAPOLEON FISH**, FOR EXAMPLE...

GO STRAIGHT TO GET TO TRAFALGAR!

ROLLING ON THE FLOOR LAUGHING... HA-HA-HA!

THE *SQUIRRELFISH*...

NO, I DON'T LIVE IN TREES!

ENOUGH OF THESE NUTTY QUESTIONS!

THE *CLOWNFISH*...

A JOKE! A JOKE!

A JOKE! A JOKE!

THE *HALFMOON ANGELFISH*...

DO YOU THINK YOU'VE GOT THE HEAD OF AN ANGEL?

I'VE ALSO A HEAD FOR ASTRONOMY...

HUH?

THE *STONEFISH*...

WHY NOT MENTION *PEBBLE FISH*, WHILE WE'RE AT IT?!

THE *TRUMPETFISH*...

HEY--QUIET!

SILENCE!

SOME FOLKS'RE SLEEPING HERE!

TARATATATARATAT

I'M WORKING TOMORROW!

SILENCE!

THE *LIZARDFISH*...

♪HUHHH!♪ IT'S NOT ALWAYS EASY TO SUNBATHE UNDERWATER!

THE *LONGNOSE BUTTERFLYFISH*...

TOOT TOOT TOOT

I'M TOO GOOD TO BE IN THIS GRAPHIC NOVEL!

THAT ONE'S MISS SNOOTY LONGNOSE!

HA-HA!

COME ON, GOOD CITIZENS! IT'S NOT WORTH GETTING WORKED UP OVER SOMETHING SO SMALL!

WHO'S THAT?

THE *EMPEROR ANGELFISH*!

UH, WELL, AT LEAST THERE'S SOMEONE WHO'S ACTUALLY HAPPY WITH HIS NAME!

EVER HIGHER, EVER FARTHER! EXCELSIOR!

THE ARROW CRAB

I'VE SEEN YOU BEFORE... BUT I CAN'T REMEMBER WHERE! YOU'RE A SPIDER-THINGIE-THINGAMABOB, RIGHT?

TOTALLY WRONG!

I'M CALLED AN *ARROW CRAB!*

HMM...THAT DOESN'T TELL ME ANYTHING...

WELL... WHEN I HUNT, I USE MY ROSTRUM...

...LIKE AN *ARROW!*

SHRUNT

I WAIT UNTIL IT'S DEAD TO EAT IT...

I KNOW YOU, BUT NOT BECAUSE OF THIS ARROW STORY...

AIEEEEEE...

OKAY, THEN. I'LL GIVE YOU A CLUE: *"THEY SAY I'M A HECK OF A MONUMENT!"*

OH, YES! THAT'S IT!

POP

PUFF

YOU'RE THE ONE THAT'S ALSO CALLED THE *EIFFEL TOWER CRAB!*

WELL, LOOKY HERE--

--HERE COME THE TOURISTS!

ARROW CRAB
Stenorhynchus seticornis

- SIZE: 5-10 centimeters [2-4 inches]

- DIET: Detritivore and carnivore

- DISTINCTIVE FEATURE: It's also called the Yellowline Arrow Crab or even Johnny Boy if you're friends with it.

| DEPTH: 1-20 METERS [0-66 FEET] | NE* | GEOGRAPHIC LOCATION |

*THREATENED SPECIES RATING. SEE THE TABLE ON PAGE TWO.

WHAT ARE FINS FOR?

EVERY FIN HAS ITS USE...

...YOU CAN TAKE NOTES!

CAUDAL

DORSAL

ANAL

PECTORAL

PELVIC

THE DORSAL FIN, LIKE THE ANAL, IS USED TO TURN AND ALSO TO STOP SUDDENLY!

LIKE THAT, EH?

FEEEEEEE

IN ADDITION TO BEING A RUDDER, THE CAUDAL FIN ALSO LETS IT ZOOM AWAY!

VROOOM VROOOM...

THE PELVIC AND PECTORAL FINS ARE THERE TO STABILIZE AND SLOW DOWN--

AUTOPILOT, WHAT?!

AND THEN THERE ARE THE OTHER FINS WHICH HAVE DIFFERENT USES, DEPENDING ON THE SPECIES...

NAVIGATIONAL AID...

COURTSHIP DISPLAY...

TURN SIGNAL...

SAY HELLO!

AAHHHHHH!

?

LOOK OUT!

AAHHHH!

VRROOOMMM

THE CAUDAL FIN IS FOR *ACCELERATING,* NOT FOR *BRAKING!* YOU'VE FAILED!

≷GULP!≷ I'M NEXT... I HOPE HE WON'T ASK ME TO PARALLEL PARK...!

YEAH... THAT EXAMINER'S TOUGH!

GA-GA...

23

THE ANILOCRA

DDTZZZ ZAP TZZZ TZZZ ZAP

UNH–UNH... IT'S A CRUSTACEAN THAT'S **GOT** PARASITES!

IT LOVES TO SUCK THE BLOOD OF FISH...

WOULD YOU MIND **ASKING** FIRST?

SHMAP

WHEN TWO ANILOCRAS CLING TO THE SAME ANIMAL...

SORRY-- ALREADY TAKEN!

RE-SHMAP

...THEY CAN COMMUNICATE WITH EACH OTHER...

HELLO, I HAVEN'T SEEN YOU FOR AGES!

EEEEKK

I WAS PART OF A **WRASSE**, BUT I WANTED A CHANGE...

...AND EVEN SEE EACH OTHER MORE INTIMATELY...

STOP SMOOCHING ON MY BACK!

KISS KISS KISS

THAT'S **DISGUSTING!**

WE UNDERSTAND IT'S ANNOYING FOR THE FISH INVOLVED...

AND THEN BLAHBLAHBLAHBLAH BLAHBLAHBLAHBLAH

BLAHBLAHBLAH BLAHBLAHBLAH...

MERCY!

...BUT IT'S REALLY UNBEARABLE FOR ONE SPECIES IN PARTICULAR...

AAAAAAAAARRR RRR RRR

THE LOCAL **"BASS."**

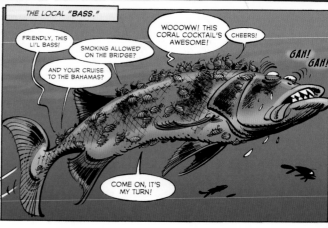

FRIENDLY, THIS LI'L BASS!

SMOKING ALLOWED ON THE BRIDGE?

AND YOUR CRUISE TO THE BAHAMAS?

WOOOWW! THIS CORAL COCKTAIL'S AWESOME!

CHEERS!

GAH! GAH!

COME ON, IT'S MY TURN!

BIOLUMINESCENCE

BIOLUMINESCENCE IS A CHEMICAL REACTION THAT PRODUCES LIGHT!

DARN... WHERE'S THE SWITCH?!

CLICK
BZZZ
CLICK
BZZZ

LOOK! THE **FLASHLIGHT FISH** AND ITS LIGHT ORGAN, LOCATED UNDER ITS EYES...

CLICK

AH, THERE IT IS!

SIDE-LIGHTS
HEADLIGHTS
HIGH BEAMS

THIS PHENOMENON HAS SEVERAL FUNCTIONS TO ATTRACT PREY FOR THE **DEEP-SEA ANGLERFISH**...

HERE LITTLE-FISHIES...

WOW!

VERY NICE...!

...TO REPEL PREDATORS FOR THE **FIRE-BREATHING SHRIMP**...

GARRGHE...THAT'S DISGUSTING!

AHH—

CHOO!

...TO CAMOUFLAGE ITSELF, LIKE THE **SQUID** THAT HAS ADAPTED ITS LUMINOSITY TO ITS ENVIRONMENT...

WELL, I'LL BE DARNED! WASN'T THERE A SQUID RIGHT AROUND HERE?

...TO ENCOURAGE MATING, LIKE THE FEMALE **PYROPHORES** WHOSE LIGHT ATTRACTS MALES!

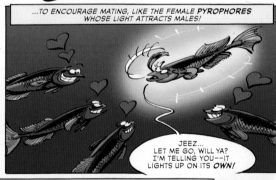

JEEZ... LET ME GO, WILL YA? I'M TELLING YOU--IT LIGHTS UP ON ITS **OWN**!

BUT IT HAS ANOTHER FUNCTION THAT MAKES ALL THESE SPECIES VERY POPULAR...

IT'S HERE!

IT GIVES PARTY NIGHTS AN AMBIANCE TO DIE FOR!

COOL!

THE ORANGE BAND SURGEONFISH

HERE'S THE **ACANTHURUS OLIVACEUS**...

WOW! A DOUBLE-BARRELED NAME! HA-HA-HA!

IT LIVES PRIMARILY IN THE WATERS OF THE PACIFIC...

ON THE CONTRARY, IT'S NOT VERY PACIFIC, HONESTLY!

LOOK HERE!

AS THEY AGE, THE MALES DEVELOP A FRONTAL BUMP...

OUCH! TAKE IT EASY WITH THOSE ROCKS FOR A BIT! YOU'LL LOOK LIKE QUASIMODO EVENTUALLY!

...IT'S CALLED THE ORANGE BAND SURGEONFISH. IT'S JUST CALLED GENDARME IN FRENCH, WHICH MEANS ARMED GUARD.

SOME PEOPLE CALL HIM, "GENERAL!"...

ATTENTION!

COULD YOU TELL ME WHAT THEY'RE DOING?

THEY HAVE TO WAIT UNTIL HE TELLS THEM, "AT EASE!"

COURTSHIP

COURTSHIP IS AN IMPORTANT PART OF LIFE...

♪♪

VROOM VROOM HEH-HEH!

FOR THE **SEAHORSE**, IT TAKES THE FORM OF A BALLET THAT CAN LAST FOR HOURS...

VROOM VROOM

PLEASE TELL ME THAT'S YOUR LAST TOUR THERE, CHAMP?!

THE **MANDARINFISH** COURT IN THE STYLE OF A "TANGO DANCER"...

CARLITO, YOOO MAKE MY E-HEAD ESPIN!

MY DEAR, YOOO'A BORN A DANCER!

THE **YASHA GOBY** BUILDS ITS BURROW AND INVITES OTHERS TO COME VISIT...

WILL YOU COME SEE ME? I NEED SOME... DECORATING ADVICE!

YEAH, SURE-- I'VE HEARD THAT ONE BEFORE!

THE **SHARK** ATTRACTS THE FEMALE'S ATTENTION BY RUBBING HER...

SORRY!

RUB RUB

SORRY!

OOPS!

HEH-HEH!

HELLO, I'M **ENZO**... AND YOU?

AS FOR THE **STICKLEBACK**, THE MALES' STOMACH TURNS RED IN ORDER TO ATTRACT FEMALES...

OLÉÉE

WOWZA-- WHAT A BELLY!

IF, DESPITE ALL THAT, THE MALE DOESN'T MANAGE TO CLINCH THE DEAL...

SO, ON THIS STARRY NIGHT--

...HE'S STILL HAS SOME OLD TECHNIQUES!

--DO YOU SEE THE CONSTELLATION OF CANCER OVER THERE?

OH, MY--YOU KNOW SO MUCH ABOUT THINGS! TEE-HEE!

27

THE GIANT SQUID'S EGGS

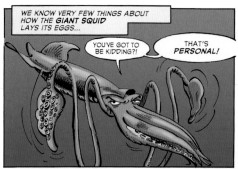

WE KNOW VERY FEW THINGS ABOUT HOW THE **GIANT SQUID** LAYS ITS EGGS...

YOU'VE GOT TO BE KIDDING?!

THAT'S **PERSONAL!**

BUT APPARENTLY WHILE MOST FISH LET THEIR EGGS FLOAT WHEREVER THEY WANT...

AND BE CAREFUL WHILE CROSSING!

SNIFF

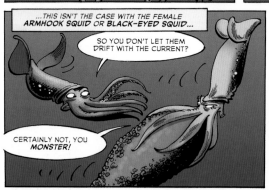

...THIS ISN'T THE CASE WITH THE FEMALE **ARMHOOK SQUID** OR **BLACK-EYED SQUID**...

SO YOU DON'T LET THEM DRIFT WITH THE CURRENT?

CERTAINLY NOT, YOU **MONSTER!**

...WHICH CARRIES HER MASS OF EGGS IN HER ARMS!

THEY WANT TO STAY WITH THEIR MOM!

RIGHT, MY DARLINGS?

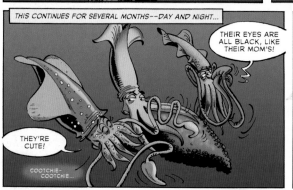

THIS CONTINUES FOR SEVERAL MONTHS--DAY AND NIGHT...

THEIR EYES ARE ALL BLACK, LIKE THEIR MOM'S!

THEY'RE CUTE!

COOTCHIE-COOTCHIE...

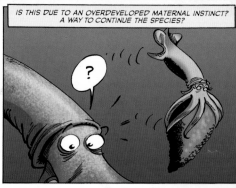

IS THIS DUE TO AN OVERDEVELOPED MATERNAL INSTINCT? A WAY TO CONTINUE THE SPECIES?

?

NO, THAT REALLY HAS NOTHING TO DO WITH THIS--!

MY MATE IS NOTHING BUT A **BIG LAZYBONES**--

--AND SHE'S FOUND A WAY TO AVOID DOING THE **SHOPPING!**

UH-OH... BUSTED!

THE STURDY TARDIGRADE!

THE **TARDIGRADE** IS ONE OF THE TOUGHEST ANIMALS ON EARTH...

THE PROOF IS AT I'M ALL OVER THE WORLD--

--EVEN IN WATER AT 4000 M [13123 FT] DEEP!

YEAH, BABY!

MEASURES 1 MM [.04 IN.]

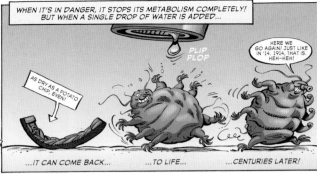

WHEN IT'S IN DANGER, IT STOPS ITS METABOLISM COMPLETELY! BUT WHEN A SINGLE DROP OF WATER IS ADDED...

PLIP PLOP

HERE WE GO AGAIN! JUST LIKE IN '14, 1914, THAT IS. HEH-HEH!

AS DRY AS A POTATO CHIP, EVEN!

...IT CAN COME BACK... ...TO LIFE... ...CENTURIES LATER!

WE'VE TESTED IT UNDER EXTREME CONDITIONS, SUBJECTED IT TO RADIATION...

GO ON, GUYS, I **LOVE** SUNBATHING!

BZZZZ!!

ECHO FROM BELOW

TOXIC PRODUCTS...

HMMM... YUM-YUM... QUITE TASTY!

IT'S BEEN PUT UNDER PRESSURE, IN A VACUUM...

HEY, DUDE, DOESN'T THIS ROCK?

?

...IN VERY LOW TEMPERATURES...

WHO LEFT THE DOOR OPEN AGAIN?

WE'VE EVEN BOILED IT AND IT STILL SURVIVES!

JUMP IN, FRIENDS--IT'S **AWESOME!**

WELL, THEN--HOW ABOUT THESE IDEAS?

?

WE COULD HAVE A REALLY **POISONOUS STONEFISH** STING YOU, EH?

HEE HEE HEE HEE

OR THROW YOU INTO THE GASTRIC JUICE OF A **GREAT WHITE SHARK!**

OR IN A DIVER'S PANTS!

HA, YOURSELVES! ENOUGH WITH ALL OF YOUR TESTS! YOU MAY LEAVE ME ALONE NOW!

OH, YEAH... JUST TO SEE YOUR REACTIONS!

HA-HA-HA!

TAP TAP TAP

THE FLYING FISH

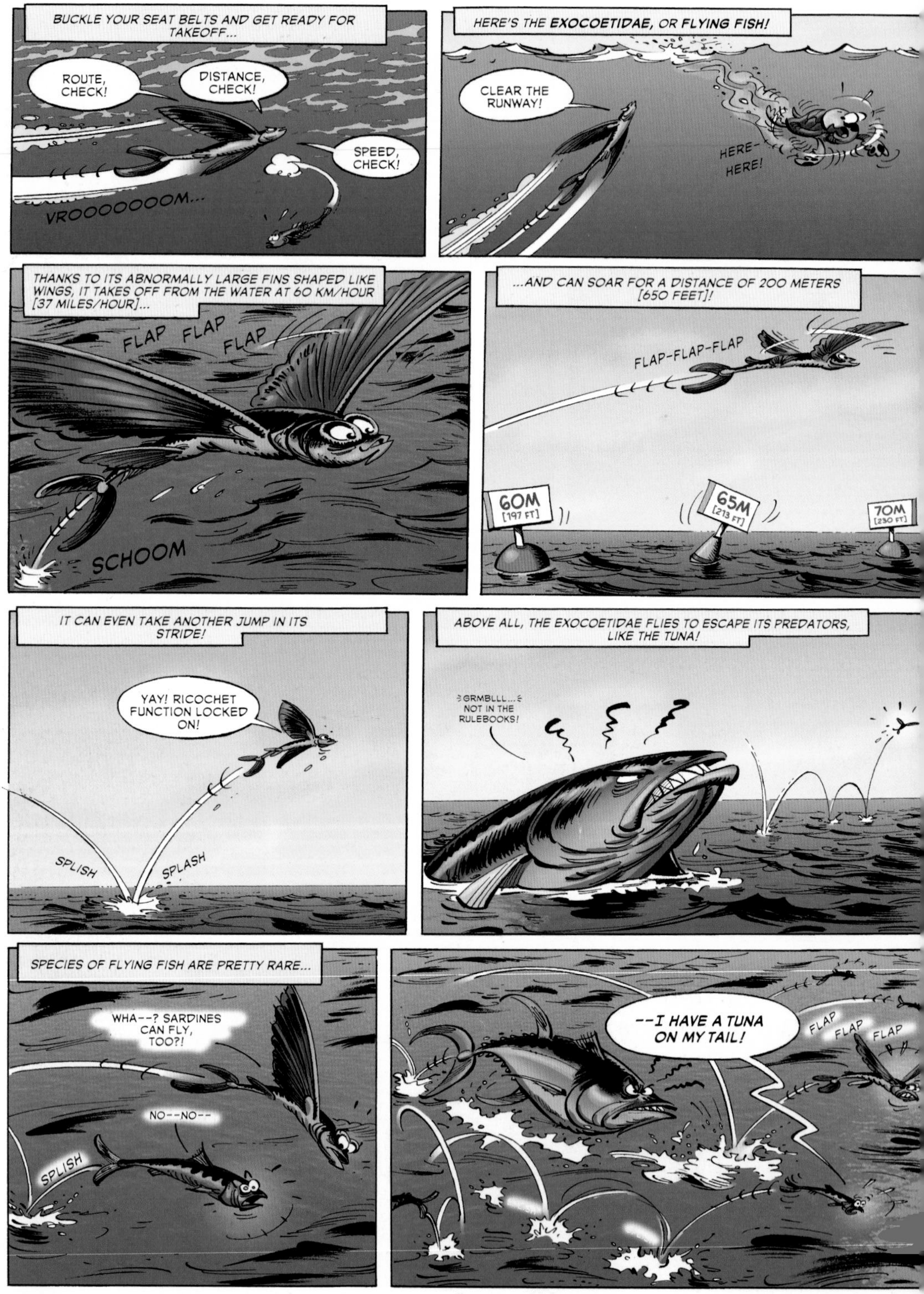
BUCKLE YOUR SEAT BELTS AND GET READY FOR TAKEOFF...
ROUTE, CHECK!
DISTANCE, CHECK!
SPEED, CHECK!
VROOOOOOOM...
HERE'S THE EXOCOETIDAE, OR FLYING FISH!
CLEAR THE RUNWAY!
HERE- HERE!
THANKS TO ITS ABNORMALLY LARGE FINS SHAPED LIKE WINGS, IT TAKES OFF FROM THE WATER AT 60 KM/HOUR [37 MILES/HOUR]...
FLAP FLAP FLAP
SCHOOM
...AND CAN SOAR FOR A DISTANCE OF 200 METERS [650 FEET]!
FLAP-FLAP-FLAP
60M [197 FT]
65M [213 FT]
70M [230 FT]
IT CAN EVEN TAKE ANOTHER JUMP IN ITS STRIDE!
YAY! RICOCHET FUNCTION LOCKED ON!
SPLISH
SPLASH
ABOVE ALL, THE EXOCOETIDAE FLIES TO ESCAPE ITS PREDATORS, LIKE THE TUNA!
GRMBLLL... NOT IN THE RULEBOOKS!
SPECIES OF FLYING FISH ARE PRETTY RARE...
WHA--? SARDINES CAN FLY, TOO?!
NO--NO--
SPLISH
--I HAVE A TUNA ON MY TAIL!
FLAP FLAP FLAP

THE BEAUTY OF THE DUGONG

HERE'S THE **SEA COW!**

HEY, YOU! MY REAL NAME IS **DUGONG!**

GOT IT?!

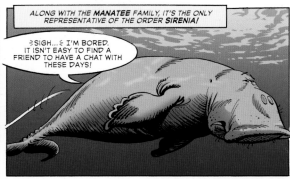

ALONG WITH THE **MANATEE** FAMILY, IT'S THE ONLY REPRESENTATIVE OF THE ORDER **SIRENIA!**

≶SIGH...≶ I'M BORED. IT ISN'T EASY TO FIND A FRIEND TO HAVE A CHAT WITH THESE DAYS!

IN THE PAST, THIS 900-KG, 4-METER-LONG--[1984 LB, 13-FT] MAMMAL USED TO LIVE IN THE ATLANTIC, AS WELL...

900KG [1984 LB]?!

WELL, THAT'S ABOUT 225 KG/METER [153 LB/FT]...

HEE!

BUT AFTER OVER-HUNTING BY HUMANS, NOW IT CAN ONLY BE FOUND IN THE INDIAN AND PACIFIC OCEANS...

THERE'RE WORSE VIEWS, DON'T YOU THINK?

SAILORS OF ANTIQUITY WERE ALWAYS IMPRESSED WHEN THEY BUMPED INTO ONE...

MAN OVER-BOARD!

?

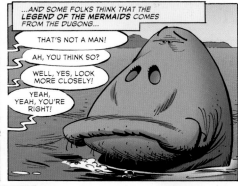

...AND SOME FOLKS THINK THAT THE **LEGEND OF THE MERMAIDS** COMES FROM THE DUGONG...

THAT'S NOT A MAN!

AH, YOU THINK SO?

WELL, YES, LOOK MORE CLOSELY!

YEAH, YEAH, YOU'RE RIGHT!

...WHICH IS CONFIRMATION FOR US THAT **GLASSES** WERE INVENTED **WELL AFTER** THE FIRST DUGONG WAS SPOTTED!

OOO-LA-LA!

DUGONG
Dugong dugon

·SIZE: 3-4 meters [10-13 feet]

·DIET: Herbivore and reef scavenger

·DISTINCTIVE FEATURE: It spends 1-8 minutes underwater per dive, because it needs to breathe from time to time.

DEPTH: AROUND 10 METERS [33 FEET]	VU*	GEOGRAPHIC LOCATION

*THREATENED SPECIES RATING. SEE THE TABLE ON PAGE TWO.

31

THE SPOTTED PORCUPINEFISH

THE BLUEFIN TUNA AT WORK

LET'S OBSERVE THE **BLUEFIN TUNA'S** HUNTING TECHNIQUE...

FIRST SPOT A SCHOOL OF FISH!

A DOUBLE AXEL SPIN--

--AND...

KER-SPLASH

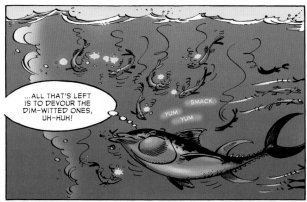

...ALL THAT'S LEFT IS TO DEVOUR THE DIM-WITTED ONES, UH-HUH!

SMACK

YUM

YUM

SECONDS!

KA-SPLOOSH

THIS TAKES GREAT CONCENTRATION...

THEN DESSERT, EH?

WHOOPS-A-DAISY!

BONG

...SINCE YOU'RE NEVER PROTECTED FROM A BAD JOKE!

HEE-HEE!

ARF-ARF!

HA-HA!

HA!

TEE-HEE!

SOUTHERN BLUEFIN TUNA
Thunnus maccoy

- SIZE: 2-3 meters [6.5-10 feet]

- DIET: Carnivore

- DISTINCTIVE FEATURE: It's so perfectly suited for swimming that American army researchers studied it to design their torpedoes.

| DEPTH: AROUND 900 METERS [2953 FEET] | CR* | GEOGRAPHIC LOCATION |

*THREATENED SPECIES RATING. SEE THE TABLE ON PAGE TWO.

THE SEAL'S WHISKERS

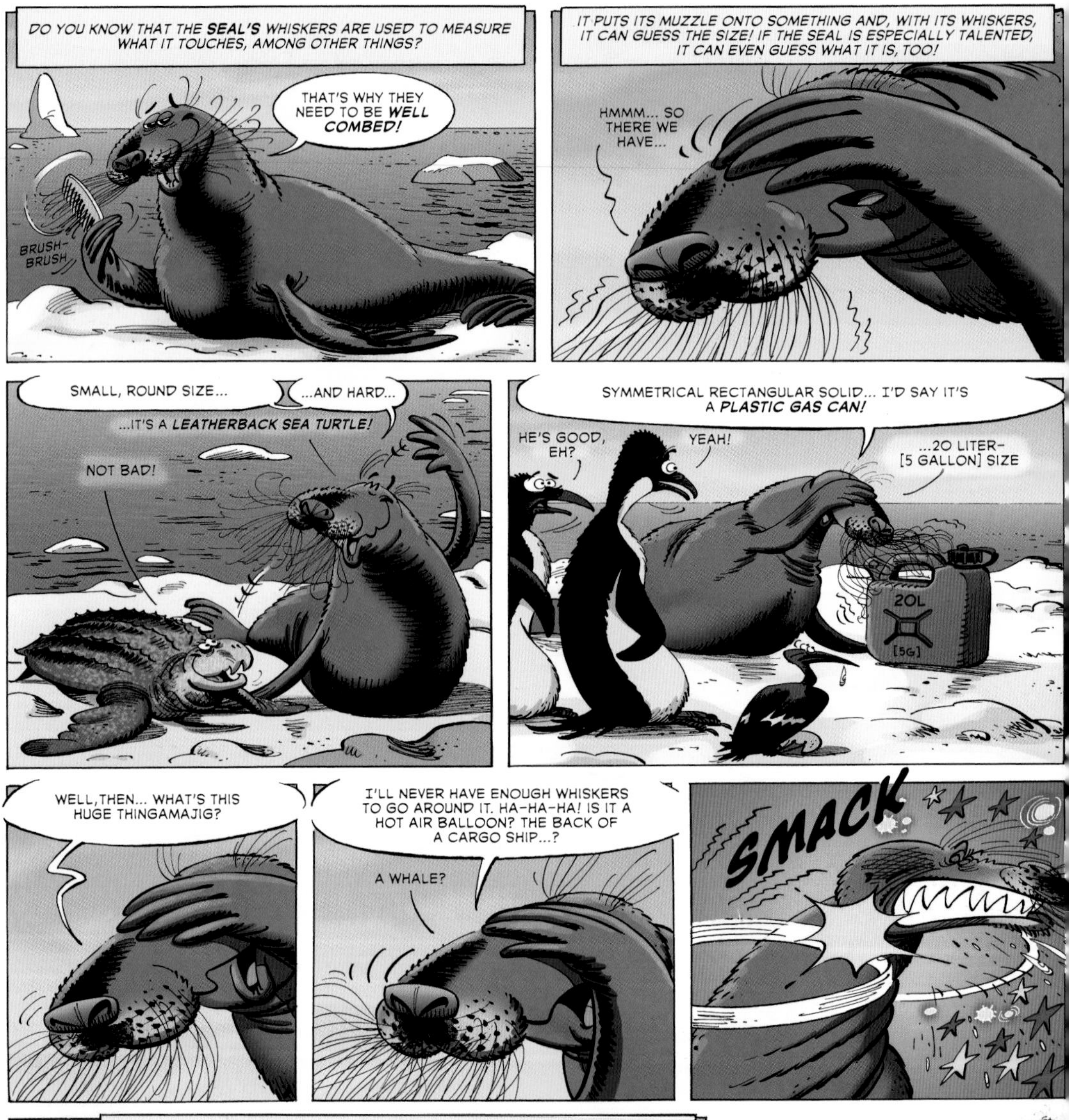
DO YOU KNOW THAT THE **SEAL'S** WHISKERS ARE USED TO MEASURE WHAT IT TOUCHES, AMONG OTHER THINGS?
THAT'S WHY THEY NEED TO BE **WELL COMBED!**
BRUSH-BRUSH
IT PUTS ITS MUZZLE ONTO SOMETHING AND, WITH ITS WHISKERS, IT CAN GUESS THE SIZE! IF THE SEAL IS ESPECIALLY TALENTED, IT CAN EVEN GUESS WHAT IT IS, TOO!
HMMM... SO THERE WE HAVE...
SMALL, ROUND SIZE...
...AND HARD...
...IT'S A *LEATHERBACK SEA TURTLE!*
NOT BAD!
SYMMETRICAL RECTANGULAR SOLID... I'D SAY IT'S A *PLASTIC GAS CAN!*
HE'S GOOD, EH?
YEAH!
...20 LITER- [5 GALLON] SIZE
20L
[5G]
WELL,THEN... WHAT'S THIS HUGE THINGAMAJIG?
I'LL NEVER HAVE ENOUGH WHISKERS TO GO AROUND IT. HA-HA-HA! IS IT A HOT AIR BALLOON? THE BACK OF A CARGO SHIP...?
A WHALE?
SMACK

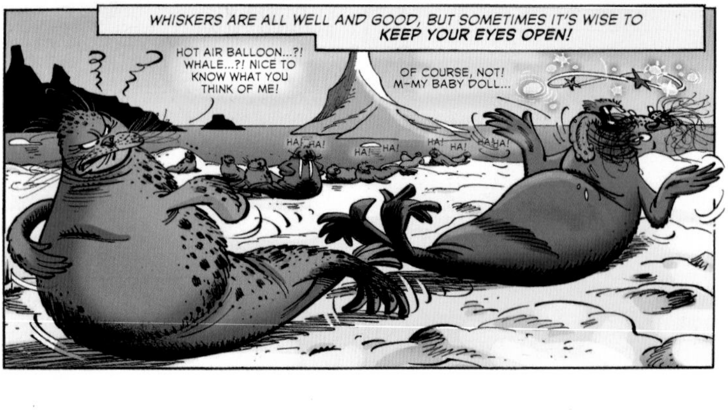
WHISKERS ARE ALL WELL AND GOOD, BUT SOMETIMES IT'S WISE TO **KEEP YOUR EYES OPEN!**
HOT AIR BALLOON...?! WHALE...?! NICE TO KNOW WHAT YOU THINK OF ME!
OF COURSE, NOT! M-MY BABY DOLL...
HA! HA! HA! HA! HA! HA! HA!

COMMON SEAL

Phoca vitulina

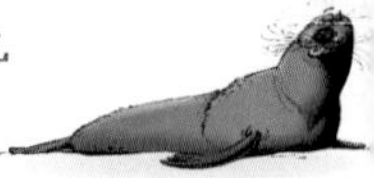

·SIZE: 1.2-1.8 meters [4-6 feet]

·DIET: Carnivore

·DISTINCTIVE FEATURE: Although it lives on dry land, it prefers to mate in the water.

DEPTH: UP TO 20 METERS [66 FEET]	LC*	GEOGRAPHIC LOCATION

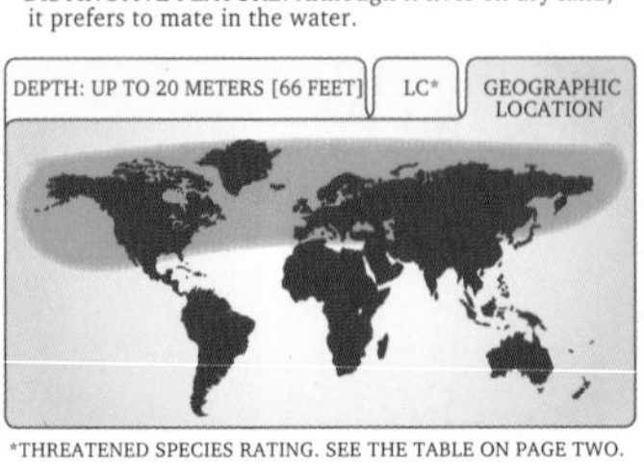

*THREATENED SPECIES RATING. SEE THE TABLE ON PAGE TWO.

THE WHALE CALF'S LICE

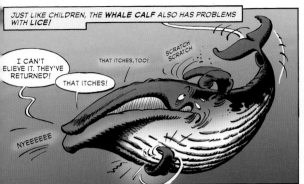

JUST LIKE CHILDREN, THE **WHALE CALF** ALSO HAS PROBLEMS WITH **LICE!**

I CAN'T BELIEVE IT. THEY'VE RETURNED!

THAT ITCHES!

THAT ITCHES, TOO!

SCRATCH SCRATCH

NYEEEEEE

THEY CLING ONTO THE FOLDS OF THE SKIN...

SCRATCH SCRATCH

COME ON, THERE'S STILL ROOM!

LUCKILY, THERE'S A DRASTIC METHOD FOR GETTING RID OF THEM...

THIS SITUATION IS **NOT** GOING TO CONTINUE!

BANZAI!

WHISH

KER-SPLASH

WOW--I'M IN SHOCK!

ARGH!

WHAT A SLAP!

ALRIGHT, IT'S **MY** TURN!

COME ON, I'M GOING TO HOLD ON FOR AT LEAST 3 MINUTES! I'M THE BEST AT **WHALE CALF-RODEO!**

IMPOSSIBLE!

WAIT, I'M GOING TO TRY, TOO!

NO ONE'S EVER DONE IT!

PHOOEY! HE WON'T EVEN HANG ON FOR A MINUTE!

AN EXAMPLE OF BIODIVERSITY

(THERE ARE MORE THAN 300 SPECIES OF ***SHARKS***)

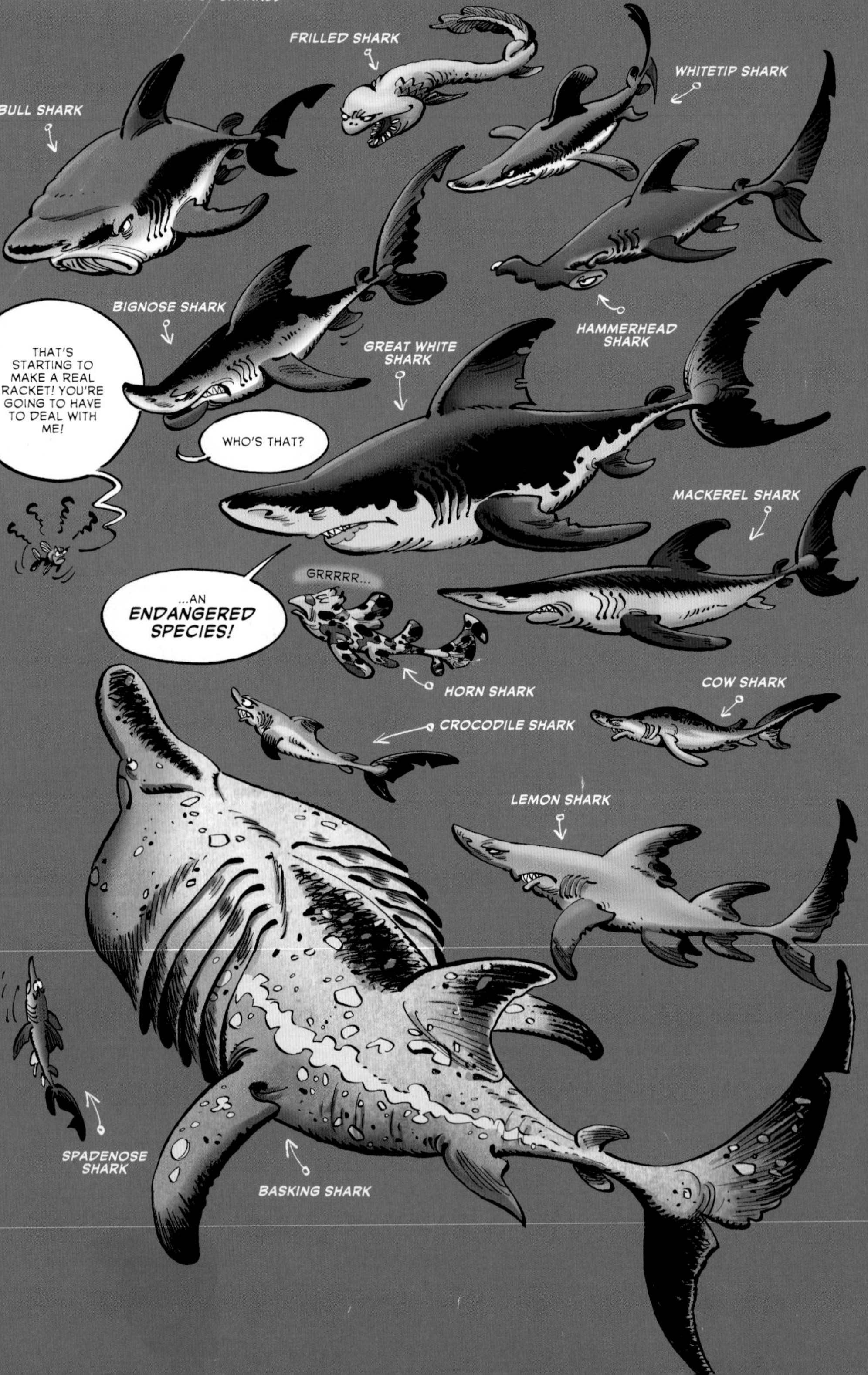

FRILLED SHARK
WHITETIP SHARK
BULL SHARK
HAMMERHEAD SHARK
BIGNOSE SHARK
THAT'S STARTING TO MAKE A REAL RACKET! YOU'RE GOING TO HAVE TO DEAL WITH ME!
GREAT WHITE SHARK
WHO'S THAT?
MACKEREL SHARK
GRRRRR...
...AN ***ENDANGERED SPECIES!***
HORN SHARK
COW SHARK
CROCODILE SHARK
LEMON SHARK
SPADENOSE SHARK
BASKING SHARK

A GAME OF DIFFERENCES

THE *SHARK* AND THE *DOLPHIN*... THAT'S LIKE *COALFISH* AND *POLLACK*. THEY'RE THE *SAME!*

WHAT? NOT AT ALL!

FOR A START, THE FIRST IS A *CARTILAGINOUS FISH* AND THE SECOND IS A *MAMMAL!*

TOOT! TOOT!

COME ON NOW, EH?

?

THE DOLPHIN IS WARM-BLOODED AND THE SHARK, COLD-BLOODED...

WOW--MY HEART SPARKS FOR YOU!

BABOOM-BABOOM-BABOOM

CALM DOWN, DARLING!

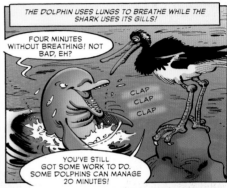

THE DOLPHIN USES LUNGS TO BREATHE WHILE THE SHARK USES ITS GILLS!

FOUR MINUTES WITHOUT BREATHING! NOT BAD, EH?

CLAP CLAP CLAP

YOU'VE STILL GOT SOME WORK TO DO. SOME DOLPHINS CAN MANAGE 20 MINUTES!

THE DOLPHIN NURSES ITS YOUNG, WHICH ISN'T THE CASE FOR THE SHARK.

...IT'S MORE ECONOMICAL THAT WAY!

SO YOU SEE, THEY'RE REALLY *OPPOSITES!*

YEAH, OKAY, THERE ARE SOME SMALL DIFFERENCES...

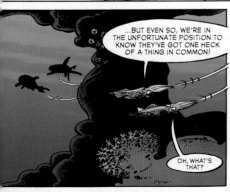

...BUT EVEN SO, WE'RE IN THE UNFORTUNATE POSITION TO KNOW THEY'VE GOT ONE HECK OF A THING IN COMMON!

OH, WHAT'S THAT?

THEY BOTH LOVE SQUID!

WHY DOESN'T ANYONE EVER TELL ME ANYTHING?!

THE PEARLFISH

I SAY, *LADY SEA CUCUMBER*, YOU DON'T LOOK VERY WELL...?

I HAVE A FISH SQUATTING INSIDE ME--IT'S A REAL *PAIN!*

INSIDE YOU?! HORRIBLE!

HOW DID IT GET THERE?

WELL, A *FIERASFER* LIKES TO ENTER THROUGH THE BACKDOOR, SO TO SPEAK!

NYYYHHH!

SOMETIMES UP TO SEVEN OF THEM ARE INSIDE ME AT ONCE! THEY'RE PROTECTED FROM THEIR PREDATORS...

...BUT I NEVER SIGNED UP FOR THIS!

THESE *"THERMOMETER FISH"* ARE MOST UNWELCOME, FOR THE OBVIOUS REASON...

YOU AMAZE ME!

OH, YEAH?! DON'T COMPLAIN TOO MUCH--

--BECAUSE AS SOON AS YOU CATCH A COLD, THEY'RE HEADED OFF TO RIO!

???

AH-CHOO AH-CHOO

OH, DON'T GO NEAR *HIM*--HE'S SICK!

YOU'RE RIGHT--IT'S NOT *CLEAN* INSIDE THERE!

THE SEAHORSE

THE **SEAHORSE** IS SUCH A BIZARRE ANIMAL!

AND NOT JUST A LITTLE BIT, EITHER!

ALWAYS ATTACHED BY ITS TAIL TO LIVING ALGAE OR A LEAF!

YEAH, I MUST ASK IT WHY IT DOES THAT!

LET'S NOT FORGET ITS MOUTH, WHICH IT USES LIKE A STRAW FOR SWALLOWING UP ITS PREY...

SLURRRPPPP

...AND THAT ITS EYES WORK **INDEPENDENTLY** FROM EACH ANOTHER!

YUP... LIKE THIS-- GLIP-GLIP-GLIP-GLIP!

ARF-ARF!

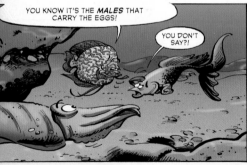

YOU KNOW IT'S THE **MALES** THAT CARRY THE EGGS!

YOU DON'T SAY?!

WHAT OUR FRIENDS FORGOT TO STATE IS THAT THE SEAHORSE TRAVELS AT A RATE OF 25 CM [.8 IN.] IN 5 MINUTES...

RIGHT, I'VE HAD IT--

--I'M LEAVING!

ME, TOO!

NICE TALKING WITH YOU ALL.

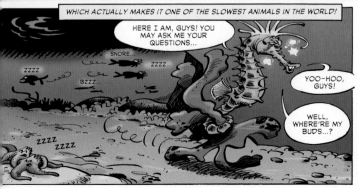

WHICH ACTUALLY MAKES IT ONE OF THE SLOWEST ANIMALS IN THE WORLD!

HERE I AM, GUYS! YOU MAY ASK ME YOUR QUESTIONS...

SNORE...

ZZZZ

ZZZZ...

BZZZ...

YOO-HOO, GUYS!

WELL, WHERE'RE MY BUDS...?

SEAHORSE
Hippocampus hystrix

·SIZE: 6-15 centimeters [2.4-6 inches]

·DIET: Carnivore

·DISTINCTIVE FEATURE: When born the young are exact replicas of their parents, except that they're smaller than 1 centimeter [.4 inches]

| DEPTH: 5-80 METERS [16-263 FEET] | NE* | GEOGRAPHIC LOCATION |

*THREATENED SPECIES RATING. SEE THE TABLE ON PAGE TWO.

ADAPTATION TO THE ENVIRONMENT

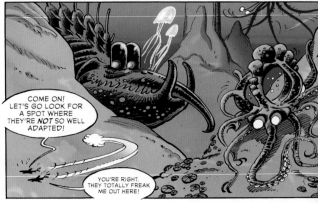

CAMOUFLAGE CHAMPION

OH, WOE IS ME!
?
WHAT'S WRONG?
THERE'S THIS HORRIBLE FEMALE WHO'S TRACKING ME. I'M LOOKING FOR A HIDING PLACE BUT I CAN'T FIND ONE!
THAT'S GREAT!
I'M A CHAMPION AT CAMOUFLAGE. YOU COULDN'T HAVE BEEN LUCKIER!
OH, REALLY?
LOOK! I COLLECT SHELLS AND PIECES OF ALGAE WITH THE PODIAS LOCATED BETWEEN MY SPINES...
?
POP
POP
POP
I COVER UP MY BODY WITH THEM AND VIOLÁ! I'M INVISIBLE! WELL, THEN?
AH, YEAH, SUPER! BUT I CAN'T DO THAT!
YOO-HOOOO!
WHOA. GOOD GRIEF-- THERE SHE IS AGAIN!
DON'T WORRY, I HAVE AN IDEA!
WHERE ARE YOOOOU, MY LOVE?!
SEE? DRESSED UP AS A SEA URCHIN, YOU GO COMPLETELY UNNOTICED!
ARGH!

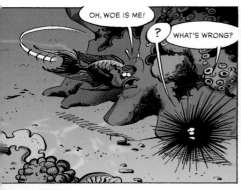

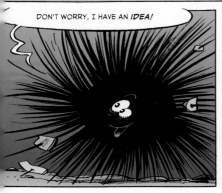

THE MUCUS OF THE DISCUS FISH

IT'S HARD BEING A PARENT! HOW DO YOU FIND FOOD FOR YOUR YOUNG WHILE KEEPING THEM SAFE?

VERY KIND OF YOU TO WATCH THEM FOR ME!

WHATEVER YOU DO, TAKE YOUR TIME!

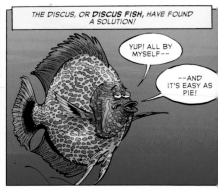

THE DISCUS, OR **DISCUS FISH,** HAVE FOUND A SOLUTION!

YUP! ALL BY MYSELF--

--AND IT'S EASY AS PIE!

THE FATHER, LIKE THE MOTHER, SECRETS A MUCUS ON ITS SCALES...

KIDS, THE MUCUS IS READY!

DINNER'S READY!

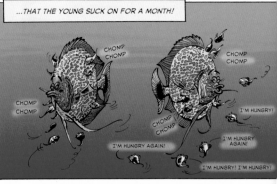

...THAT THE YOUNG SUCK ON FOR A MONTH!

CHOMP CHOMP

CHOMP CHOMP

CHOMP CHOMP

CHOMP CHOMP

I'M HUNGRY!

I'M HUNGRY AGAIN!

I'M HUNGRY AGAIN!

I'M HUNGRY! I'M HUNGRY!

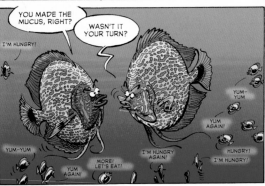

YOU MADE THE MUCUS, RIGHT?

WASN'T IT YOUR TURN?

I'M HUNGRY!

YUM-YUM

YUM AGAIN!

YUM-YUM

MORE! LET'S EAT!

I'M HUNGRY AGAIN!

HUNGRY! I'M HUNGRY!

YUM AGAIN!

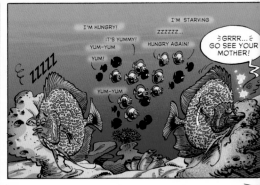

I'M HUNGRY!

I'M STARVING

ZZZZZZ...

IT'S YUMMY!

HUNGRY AGAIN!

YUM-YUM

YUM!

YUM-YUM

GRRR... GO SEE YOUR MOTHER!

ZZZZZ

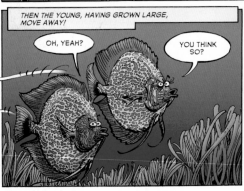

THEN THE YOUNG, HAVING GROWN LARGE, MOVE AWAY!

OH, YEAH?

YOU THINK SO?

APPARENTLY, YOU DON'T HAVE ANY CHILDREN!

DADDY, THERE'S A CONCERT AT THE CORAL TONIGHT. TAKE ME!

CAN I SPEND THE NIGHT AT THE RED MULLET'S PLACE? PRETTY PLEASE?!

THERE'S NOTHING LEFT TO EAT!

MOM, I DON'T HAVE ANYTHING TO WEAR ON MY FINS!

WHERE'S MY ALLOWANCE?

THE BANDED ARCHERFISH'S SPIT

THEY'RE PRETTY PLUMP, AREN'T THEY? BUT A LITTLE OUT OF OUR REACH...

MAYBE FOR THE *NORTHERN TROUT GUDGEON*, BUT NOT FOR A *BANDED ARCHERFISH!*

YOU'LL SEE... I PUT MYSELF RIGHT UNDERNEATH IT VERTICALLY...

AND...

SPLOOTCH

?

PING

SPLITCH

AMAZING! WHAT SNIPER PRECISION!

HMMM?

CRUNCH
CRUNCH
CRUNCH

HMMMPHH

YOU KNOW, IT'S NOT PRECISION THAT COUNTS...

CRACK

SPLOOTCH

HEE-HEE-HEE!

I SEE, IT'S IMPORTANT TO *GAUGE* YOUR STRENGTH, RIGHT?

BANDED ARCHERFISH

Toxotes jaculatrix

·SIZE: Up to 30 centimeters [12 inches]

·DIET: Insectivore

·DISTINCTIVE FEATURE: Each of its water jets is ten times as powerful as necessary, in order to be certain to dislodge its prey.

DEPTH: SHALLOW [SURFACE]	LC*	GEOGRAPHIC LOCATION

*THREATENED SPECIES RATING. SEE THE TABLE ON PAGE TWO.

THE ANTENNARIUS

THE ANTENNARIUS IS ALSO CALLED THE FROGFISH OR TOADFISH OR GIANT FROGFISH!

BUT YOU MAY CALL ME MIGUEL!

IT ATTRACTS ITS PREY BY WAVING A LURE LOCATED ON TOP OF ITS HEAD, LIKE THE MONKFISH...

HEY, YOU'VE GOT SOME HAIR STICKING OUT! HA-HA!

ARF-ARF! YEAH, THAT STYLE'S A LITTLE OUT OF DATE!

DEPENDING ON THE SPECIES, THE LURE CAN TAKE DIFFERENT FORMS--A WORM...

WOW--THAT WORM'S A BEAUTY!

IT'S MINE!

...A SHRIMP, FOR THE GIANT FROGFISH...

MOM?! WHAT'RE YOU DOING HERE?

...A LITTLE FISH FOR THE WARTY FROGFISH...

DINNERRRR'S SERVED!

DINNERRRR'S SERVED!

...OR A CRAB FOR THE THREE-SPOT FROGFISH!

CHICK CHICK...

THE ANTENNARIUS ALSO HAS A RESCUE LURE AT ITS DISPOSAL...

YOO-HOOOOO... WHERE ARE YOOOOU, MY LOVE?!

...THAT'S ESPECIALLY EFFECTIVE!

SNIFF

MOVED WITH NO FORWARDING ADDRESS

THE BURROWING URCHIN

THERE IT IS--A *BURROWING URCHIN!*

THAT'S A CLEVER NAME!

CRRR... CRRR... CRRR...

WELL, IT'S CALLED THAT BECAUSE IT DIGS OUT ITS HIDING PLACE IN A ROCK--

CRRR... CRRR... CRRR...

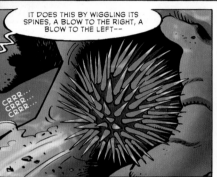

IT DOES THIS BY WIGGLING ITS SPINES, A BLOW TO THE RIGHT, A BLOW TO THE LEFT--

CRRR... CRRR... CRRR...

CRRR... CRRR... CRRR... CRRR...

THOSE SPINES MUST BE AWFULLY STURDY--

I IMAGINE SO!

OF COURSE, IT DOESN'T DO THIS WITH A SNAP OF A CLAW--IT TAKES TIME!

A LOT OF TIME!

CRRR... CRRR... CRRR...

FASCINATING!

CRRR... CRRR... CRRR...

NAH, NOT REALLY!

CRRR...

NOT WHEN YOU LIVE NEXT TO A HOME OF SEA URCHINS THAT'S UNDER *CONSTRUCTION!*

OH, YEAH!

BOO-HOO! I'VE HAD IT!

CRRR... CRRR... CRRR... CRRR... CRRR... CRRR... CRRR... CRRR... CRRR...

BURROWING SEA URCHIN
Echinometra mathaei

·SIZE: 5-20 centimeters [2-8 inches]

·DIET: Omnivore

·DISTINCTIVE FEATURE: It can shelter different species of shrimp between its spikes

| DEPTH: UP TO 140 METERS [459 FEET] | NE* | GEOGRAPHIC LOCATION |

*THREATENED SPECIES RATING. SEE THE TABLE ON PAGE TWO.

A SPECIAL CASE

BLUBB-BLUBB

?

AHOY! CAN YOU HEAR ME ON THE BOAT? I'VE JUST SPOTTED A *JELLYFISH* FROM AN *UNIDENTIFIED SPECIES!* I'M FOLLOWING IT...!

IT LETS ITSELF BE CARRIED BY THE CURRENTS WITHOUT TRYING TO DIRECT ITSELF... NO IMPETUS...

WHAT GRACE!

INTERESTING--IT DOESN'T AROUSE THE APPETITE OF THE TURTLE, WHICH GENERALLY IS A GOURMAND! MAYBE IT'S TOXIC TO THEM?

CLICK CLICK

IT'S AMAZING! ORDER AN OBSERVATION SUBMARINE WITH VIDEO EQUIPMENT...

DON'T WORRY ABOUT THE COST...

WE'RE LOOKING AT THE DISCOVERY OF THE CENTURY!

CLICK CLICK CLICK

DO YOU THINK HE KNOWS IT'S A *PLASTIC BAG?*

LET THE HUMAN GO-- HE'S LEAVING US IN PEACE!

BRILLIANT! UNIQUE! EXTRAORDINARY!

CLICK CLICK CLICK

PLASTIC BAG
Saccus plasticus

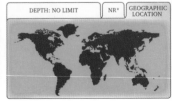

·SIZE: 45 centimeters long by 26 centimeters wide [18 inches long by 10 inches wide]

·DIET: Litterer

·DISTINCTIVE FEATURE: It pollutes, kills, and creates plastic continents, all due to human carelessness

DEPTH: NO LIMIT	NR*	GEOGRAPHIC LOCATION

*NOT AT RISK!

WATCH OUT FOR PAPERCUTZ

Ahoy! Welcome aboard the soggy, semi-scientific, second SEA CREATURES IN THEIR OWN WORDS graphic novel by Christophe Cazenove and Thierry Jytéry from Papercutz, those sea-faring scallywags dedicated to publishing great graphic novels for all ages. I'm Jim Salicrup, Editor-in-Chief and part-time Fish Whisperer. But I'm here with a really BIG ANNOUNCEMENT…

The really BIG ANNOUNCEMENT is that Papercutz is launching a whole new line of graphic novels, filled with exciting characters, a big dose of romance, with great writing and artwork. The new line of titles is called Charmz, and we suspect you're going to love each and every Charmz title, because they're totally irresistible!

Now you might be thinking, how can there be anything more exciting than a graphic novel filled with talking fish telling us all about their interesting lives? Well, have you checked out the Papercutz series called DINOSAURS, which featured prehistoric creatures spouting factoids about their fascinating lives? We're not necessarily saying that *that's* more exciting, just different and equally exciting in its own way… Just like the Charmz titles.

Take STITCHED, for example. Crimson Volania wakes up one day, and probably would tell you all about her strange life, except she can't remember anything about it! Nor does she know where she is and the strange characters she starts encountering. It appears she's in a cemetery and the folks she keeps running into include a spooky whirlwind of ghosts, werewolves, witches, and weirdly beautiful boys. Now, despite not knowing who she is, she manages to develop a big time crush on one of the groovy ghoulies she meets. We'll let you guess which one!

You can find out a lot more about Charmz by going to papercutz.com. As for that graphic novel series with the gabby dinos, check out the special excerpt from DINOSAURS #2 "Bite of the Albertosaurus" on the following pages. We'll let them do the talking from this point on.

Well, except to remind you not to miss SEA CREATURES IN THEIR OWN WORDS #3 "Shell Life," coming soon to the bookstore or library near you!

Thanks,

Jim

STAY IN TOUCH!

EMAIL:	salicrup@papercutz.com
WEB:	www.papercutz.com
TWITTER:	@papercutzgn
INSTAGRAM	@papercutzgn
FACEBOOK:	PAPERCUTZGRAPHICNOVELS
REGULAR MAIL:	Papercutz, 160 Broadway, Suite 700, East Wing, New York, NY 10038

MORE GREAT GRAPHIC NOVEL SERIES AVAILABLE FROM PAPERCUTZ

SEA CREATURES #1

SEA CREATURES #2

ANNE OF GREEN BAGELS #1

DISNEY FAIRIES #18

FUZZY BASEBALL

THE GARFIELD SHOW #6

THE LUNCH WITCH #1

DINOSAURS #1

NANCY DREW DIARIES #7

THE RED SHOES

SCARLETT

THE SISTERS #1

THE WILD SMURF

GERONIMO STILTON #18

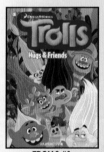
TROLLS #1

DINOSAURS WEAPONS

DINOSAURS HAD A VARIETY OF WEAPONS AT THEIR DISPOSAL FOR ATTACKING OR FOR DEFENDING THEMSELVES...

TEETH AS SHARP AS DAGGERS...

INCREDIBLY SPIKY HORNS...

RAZOR-SHARP CLAWS...

TAILS SHAPED LIKE CLUBS...

OR STRONGER THAN WHIPS...

WHEN THEY WEREN'T FULL OF SPIKES!

AND ME? YOU DIDN'T SAY ANYTHING ABOUT MY SUPER KILLING WEAPON OF DEATH?

UMM.... SORRY, COMPSO, BUT WE DON'T SEE ANYTHING!

WELL, YES, HERE'S MY WEAPON: A NICE, BIG BUDDY!

AND ADD "CRUSHING" TO THE LIST!

ARGHH...! IT'S NOT MY DAY...

DINOSAURES [Dinosaurs] by Arnaud Plumeri & Bloz © 2010 BAMBOO ÉDITION. www.bamboo.fr

49

THE EARTH IS 4.6 BILLION YEARS OLD.

THAT'S REALLY OLD!

BUT IF WE COMPRESS ITS HISTORY INTO 24 HOURS, WE'LL UNDERSTAND THINGS BETTER!

OBSERVE...

AT 0:00, THE EARTH MATERIALIZES. THE FIRST FOUR HOURS, IT FORMS AND COOLS DOWN...

NOT A HAIRBALL!

AT 4:00, THE FIRST BACTERIA APPEAR IN THE SEA...

ACHOOO!

LOT OF GERMS AROUND HERE!

AT 20:30, PLANTS MOVE INTO THE MARINE DEPTHS, FOLLOWED BY JELLYFISH.

I'M STUNNED THAT WE'D APPEAR SO LATE!

AT 22:00 PLANTS SETTLE IN ON DRY LAND, FOLLOWED BY THE FIRST INSECTS AND ANIMALS...

IN SHORT, WE GO WHERE THERE'S GRUB!

YES, I'M TALKING ABOUT YOU!

SLURP

DIMETRODON (IT'S A REPTILE, NOT A DINOSAUR!)

AT 22:59, THE FIRST DINOSAURS APPEAR.

YEAH!

AT 23:39, DINOSAURS DISAPPEAR AND MAMMALS DEVELOP.

TOLD YOU I WAS STRONGER THAN YOU!

HEE-HEE!

TICKTOCKTICKTOCKTICKTOCKTICKTOCK

TICKTOCKTOCKTIC

AT 23:59, OUR PRIMATE ANCESTORS BEGIN EVOLVING.

AND WE MODERN HUMANS ONLY APPEAR AT 23:59 AND 56 SECONDS!

SO WHAT ARE YOU TELLING ME?!

ARE YOU GOING TO BUY THIS WATCH FROM ME OR WHAT?

IT ISN'T EVEN 05:00 YET!

Cuckoo Clock Shoppe

ALBERTOSAURUS

THE ALBERTOSAURS, COUSINS OF T. REX, ARE HUNTING...

THERE WOULDN'T BE SOMETHING AROUND HERE TO MUNCH ON, WOULD THERE?

BINGO! A HERD OF CENTROSAURUS!

HORNED BEASTIES?

THEIR FAVORITE TECHNIQUE: A SURPRISE ATTACK ON THE WEAK...

CHARGE! ROAR

BUT THE CENTROSAURUS PARRY...

QUICK, GET IN A CIRCLE! PROTECT THE WEE ONES!

AND THE BATTLE QUICKLY TURNS TO CARNAGE FOR THE CARNIVORES...

SHRIIIEEEK

ROAR

LET'S GET OUT OF HERE! OUR MEALS ARE MEANIES!

OWIE OWIE!

I'M HUUUUUNGRY!

NEVER EVER TALK TO ME AGAIN ABOUT HORNED BEASTS!

WE COULD EAT SNAILS!

SLURP

ALBERTOSAURUS

MEANING: ALBERTA (CANADIAN PROVINCE) LIZARD
PERIOD: LATE CRETACEOUS (70 MILLION YEARS AGO)
ORDER/ FAMILY: SAURISCHIA/ TYRANNOSAURIDAE
SIZE: 30 FEET LONG
WEIGHT: 6,000 LBS.
DIET: CARNIVORE
FOUND: NORTH AMERICA

THE PROFESSION OF PALEONTOLOGY

EVEN WHEN HE WAS VERY LITTLE, YOUNG ARCHIBALD JONES ADORED DINOSAURS.

THROUGHOUT HIS CHILDHOOD, HE DREAMED OF DISCOVERING T. REX BONES IN THE FAMILY'S GARDEN.

WORRIED, HIS MOTHER TOOK HIM TO A PSYCHOLOGIST. AND THE VERDICT WAS...

DOCTOR, HE DIGS HOLES EVERYWHERE. IS IT GRAVE?

NOT AT ALL. HE DREAMS OF BECOMING A PALEONTOLOGIST!

PALEO-WHAT?

TO BECOME A PALEONTOLOGIST-- A SPECIALIST IN EXTINCT SPECIES-- ARCHIBALD STUDIED HARD...

TELL ME, ARCHIE, DO YOU LIKE ME?

STUDY HALL

MMM?

YOUR AMBER NECKLACE IS AWESOME! DID YOU KNOW YOU COULD FIND MOSQUITOES THAT BIT DINOSAURS IN IT?

HEY!

NEXT, SCHOOL BREAKS BECAME AN OPPORTUNITY TO WORK ON DIGS WITH PALEONTOLOGISTS.

WOW! TAKE IT EASY! YOU'RE LIKELY TO DAMAGE A FOSSIL!

PIC PIC

PIC PIC

TODAY, HE'S NICKNAMED INDINO JONES AND IS THE IDOL OF CHILDREN...

AND THEIR MOTHERS, IN FACT...

WHAT WOULD YOU SAY ABOUT HAVING DINNER WITH ME? I'M DIVORCED AND MY SON SEEMS TO ADORE YOU.

AH, YES, WE COULD HAVE FUN!

PALEONTOLOGY: MORE THAN A CAREER, IT'S A LIFELONG PASSION!

PFFFF....

ROOAR GROWWWL

PUMIER + BLOZ

T. REX'S APPETITE

HEALTH TIP: NEVER GIVE YOUR T. REX LETTUCE!

THE SIZE OF DINOSAURS

IF DINOSAURS LIVED IN OUR CITIES TODAY, WE'D HAVE A BETTER IDEA OF THEIR SIZE RIGHT AWAY!

TAKE, FOR EXAMPLE, THIS DIPLODOCUS...

...IT WOULD OVERSHADOW BUSES AND CREATE MONSTROUS TRAFFIC JAMS!

THE GALLIMIMUS WOULD PROBABLY GET A SPEEDING TICKET!

AND THE IGUANODON-- WITH ITS POINTY THUMBS-- WOULD UNDOUBTEDLY HITCHHIKE...

...BUT YOU'D HAVE TROUBLE GETTING IT INTO YOUR CAR!

EEEEEK!!

EVEN IF YOU WERE ON THE FOURTH FLOOR OF YOUR BUILDING, YOU WOULDN'T BE SAFE FROM THE PRYING EYES OF A BRACHIOSAURUS!

A TRICERATOPS WOULDN'T HAVE ANY PROBLEM FINDING A PARKING PLACE!

BLAM

FIFI!

AND YOU'D BE HARD PRESSED TO KEEP YOUR VELOCIRAPTORS ON A LEASH...

GNAP GNAP   HHISSS

TAP TAP TAP TAP

A COMPSOGNATHUS WOULD DEFINITELY FIGHT WITH THE ALLEY CATS FOR SOMETHING TO EAT!

IN SHORT, IF DINOSAURS WERE AMONG US, THEY'D EASILY FIND A MEAL THEIR SIZE...

BUT THE DISHES ON THE MENU WOULD OFTEN BE US!

DINOSAUR FEET

THIS COMPSOGNATHUS WILL HELP US EXPLAIN A METHOD FOR CLASSIFYING MOST DINOSAURS...

ARE YOU KIDDING? I'VE GOT OTHER THINGS TO DO! I'M HUNTING!

...THANKS TO THE SHAPE OF THEIR "FEET."

FOOTSTEPS... SOMEONE'S NEAR...THE POOR GUYS HAVE NO IDEA I'M GOING TO EAT THEM.

FIRST, WE SEPARATE OUT THE ORNITHOPODS (LIKE THESE DRYOSAURUS)...

...IN OTHER WORDS, DINOSAURS "WITH BIRD FEET."

OUGH! OW! NOT BIRD FEET!

NEXT, THE SAUROPODS ("LIZARD FEET"), INCLUDING LONG-NECKED DINOSAURS LIKE BRACHIOSAURUS.

NOOOO! NOT LIZARD FEET!

RATS... I'M LUCKY TO BE ALIVE...

WITHOUT FORGETTING THE THEROPODS ("BEAST FEET")...

BL OP

...A GROUP THAT INCLUDES MOST CARNIVOROUS HUNTERS, LIKE THIS ALLOSAURUS.

GRRRRR! THEY GOT AWAY FROM US!

YUCK! I STEPPED ON SOMETHING STICKY!

HAH! HAH! WE'LL CLASSIFY YOU UNDER "POOPOPODS": STINKY FEET!

PLUMERI & BLOZ

Don't Miss DINOSAURS #2 "Bite of the Albertosaurus" Available Now at Booksellers Everywhere!

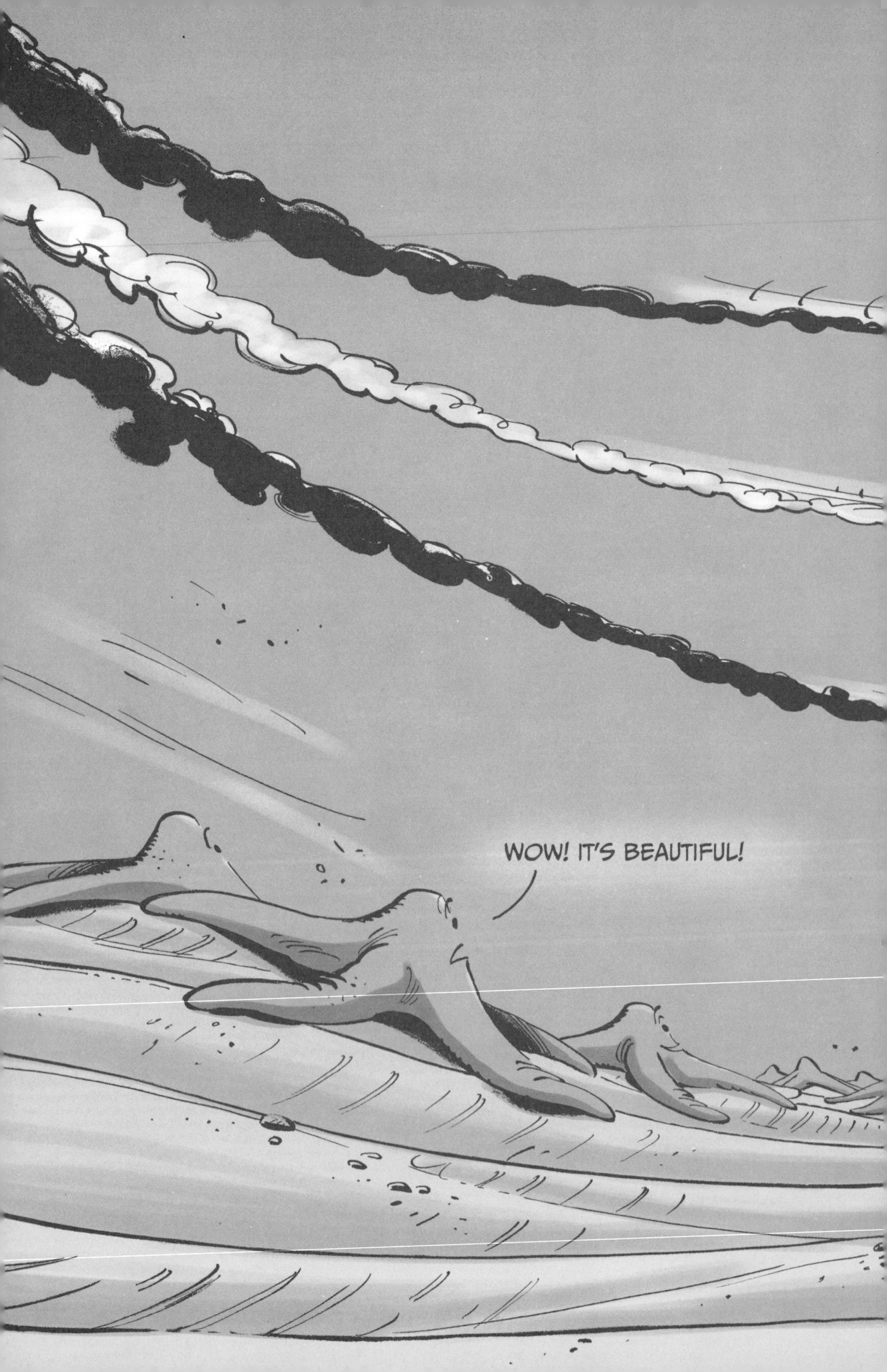
WOW! IT'S BEAUTIFUL!